ONE LAST RIDE
By Dan Elish
The truth is the best part of a man is a boy.
- Marjorie Kinnan Rawlings

One Last Ride
Copyright © 2024 by Daniel Elish

All rights reserved. This book or any portion thereof may not be reproduced or used in any manner whatsoever without the express written permission of the author, except for the use of brief quotations in a book review.

Cover by Jewelz Claypool
Editing by 10,000 Lakes Publishing
Formatting by Beth Hercules
Drawings by Wendie Moore Wilhide

Also by Dan Elish

The Worldwide Dessert Contest
Jason and the Baseball Bear
The Great Squirrel Uprising
Born Too Short
Nine Wives
The Misadventures of Justin Hearnfeld
13 (co-written with Jason Robert Brown)
The School for the Insanely Gifted
The Attack of the Frozen Woodchucks
The Royal Order of Fighting Dragons
King of Broadway
The Silver Spoon

For Doug Johnson and all my other camp friends

Chapter 1

I know I shouldn't be stopping to chill with a horse, not with most of the kids already at the dance. But halfway across the giant pasture that separates Flying Eagle (us boys) from Ruth Bader Ginsberg (them girls), I notice Merrylegs in her regular spot under the giant oak tree just below the ball field, brown coat, black mane, looking my way.

I glance at Mateo, my summer partner in camp crime. His blonde hair with purple streaks hangs to his shoulders, his jeans ripped at the knees.

"Gimme a sec," I say.

"Jackson. Come on, bro. No."

"Just a second!"

"Jackson! The dance!"

I sprint across the outfield grass—it's never mowed at

Flying Eagle, a badge of pride—and throw my arms around Merrylegs' neck.

She isn't a particularly big horse maybe even technically more of a largish pony but plenty tall for a medium-sized twelve-year-old kid like me. The most popular in Flying Eagle's stable, she never stamps her hooves in the ring or reaches for leaves on the trail no matter what sort of riding-challenged, rein-slapping, psycho is on her back. But even though her natural ease makes her pretty much everyone's favorite, she thinks I'm special—at least, that's what I like to think. I lead her in from the pasture each morning, curry and brush her before saddling, and ride her practically every day.

If that sounds like the backdrop to one of those horrible "boy loves horse" poems you were maybe forced to read in fifth grade, I plead guilty. No one was more surprised by the way that summer had gone than me. When I arrived at camp seven weeks earlier, I was a city kid from the biggest of them all. You know the one I mean: the place with the Empire State Building, Broadway shows and about a million miles of subway tracks. I had barely even seen a horse up close, let alone climbed onto one's back. Coming to an out-of-the-way, no-frills hole like Flying Eagle, I had my eye on woodshop and archery, maybe a little tennis. But when Doug Gartner, my cabin counselor, dragged me to the ranch the first week, it was love at first ride. For a kid whose previous animal experience had been limited to pigeons, squirrels, and the occasional really large rat it was a bigtime jolt. But I advanced fast. After two weeks in Group One, beginners, I got with keeping my butt in the saddle and staying short on the reins. Promoted to Group Two, I learned how to post. Six weeks into the summer, Doug put me in Group Three, advanced.

So now here I am, dressed in a freshly washed Mets t-shirt and my own pair of ripped jeans, pressing my head into Merrylegs' mane. I even give her a little kiss (yeah, I do that sometimes, so what?), then pat her back.

"Good girl."

"Jackson! Hurry up!"

Mateo again.

"I'm coming!"

Merrylegs neighs and pushes her head against my cheek. But when I hear the sound of hooves in the dirt, I know it's finally time to get out of there. Coming up from behind is Major, the strongest horse at the ranch, too rowdy for most campers to ride on the trail, too high off the ground to mount without a boost. But even though Major is a force of nature with super-natural strength, he has a soft side. We ranch regulars can tell that he's hot for Merrylegs.

Now, when I meet his dark eyes, I think I can read his mind: "Move off my woman, punk!"

It's good timing. Mateo is officially over it.

"Yo, Jackson!" he calls. "You do realize that Merrylegs is a horse? Like an animal, OK? Save some of that love for the girls."

He has a point. Time to get to the main event: the dance. Still, just for the fun of it, I'm tempted to pick up a piece of dried manure and chase Mateo around the ballfield. I've done that before, once even rubbing a piece of it into one of his purple streaks. But I hesitate. After all, even a socially challenged twelve-year-old knows it's not smart to go to a dance with dried horse crap on his fingers.

Instead, I give Merrylegs a final pat on her brown coat and watch her trot off with Major, her head tucked against his muscular dark shoulder. Then a small black and white pinto, Copper, trots to their side—he likes Merrylegs, too, I can tell—and the three of them graze while I run back to my bud.

"Okay," I call to Mateo. "Let's go."

"Good," he says. "Gonna be late!"

I'm about to point out that the reason for that has nothing to do with my desire to say a quick hello to a horse and everything to do with that fact that he had needed extra time to choose the right t-shirt (They Might Be Giants National Tour). But I keep my mouth shut and hustle after him, cutting down the pasture, past the archery range, then through a small pine forest to the wooden gate that separates the two camps. On most days, it's illegal to cross the line into female territory. But tonight, the gate is open. Steps away, the distant peal of the Ruth Bader Ginsberg bell pushes Mateo into high gear. If he's extra eager to make a grand entrance it's understandable: I mean, the kid has an actual girlfriend—you heard me: AN ACTUAL GIRLFRIEND—Patti Vost, the best looking girl in our sister cabin. They've hung out at every dance all summer. For the past week or so Mateo has held steady to his claim that they've kissed, "On the lips, dudes. For a full minute and a half."

I guess he timed it, too.

"Come on!" Mateo calls from the gate.

Just then I hear a neigh from the Flying Eagle pasture, followed by the distant pounding of hooves. Sounds like a couple of the horses burning off early evening energy. Probably Major and Copper, maybe even racing to impress Merrylegs. Who knows?

"Catch you guys on the way home!" I call over my shoulder.

"Dude!" Mateo calls. "Hurry the hell up!"

So that's what I do.

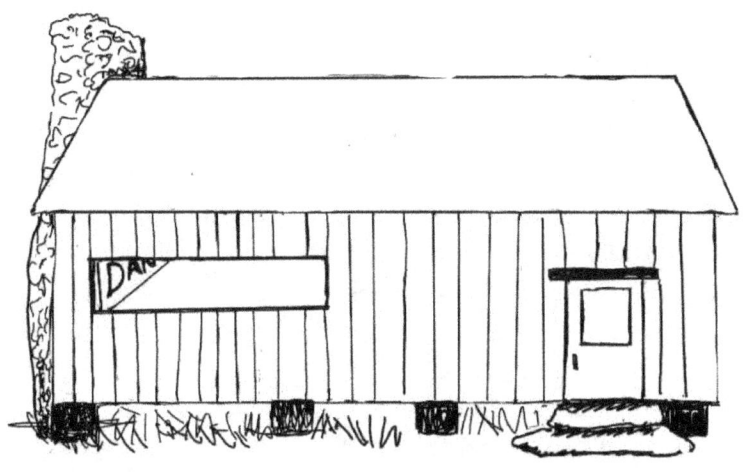

Chapter 2

"Life is full of ups and down, Jackson, unforeseen problems"—that's the line mom took a few months before camp. Maybe that wasn't the deepest thing she'd ever said, but there was truth in it because "unforeseen problems" were why I ended up at a throw-back camp like Flying Eagle in the first place. See, my parents needed some "alone time" but not the type of alone time that came with wine and a long, slow fade to the sunset. You didn't have to be a genius or a shrink or even a reasonably intelligent toddler to read between the lines of the pissed-off sighs and hard stares they traded that year. Nope, the reason my folks wanted to be alone was to see if they wanted to be together at all.

It was almost funny. At first, mom and dad tried to keep

super quiet about the real reason they were suddenly so eager to send their only child to camp. That spring mom started saying things like, "A New York kid needs time in the outdoors" and "Come on, Jackson! There's more to life than YouTube." Meanwhile, my dad got all misty-eyed with tales of his days at a place in Maine called Camp Winatooga. But I knew that dad's re-discovered love affair with camping wasn't the real reason my parents wanted to ship me off. And when I found my mom crying in the kitchen one afternoon she spilled the whole stupid mess. My parents were having troubles, she admitted. But they weren't giving up on each other. There was a lot of love there. "What can I say, Jackson?" dad said later that night. "Relationships are complicated. You've had crushes, right?"

Who hadn't? Still, truth out, I arrived at Flying Eagle that summer with very little go-to girl-experience. Of course, I had *noticed* them. I was even friendly with some girls around the school hallways and—full disclosure—I had had a recurring daydream about two I thought were cute and smart, Marilyn Ashford (Science class, good mouth, knew a ton about rocks), and Mariana Griffin (English class, nice kneecaps, quoted Steven Colbert). The way I pictured it, they were each on the US Woman's basketball team and I was a star point guard for the Knicks. At the summer Olympics we shared a hotel suite, stripped down to our underwear and compared gold medals. Nice, huh? Despite these twisted visions of love in the world of international sports, before camp that summer I couldn't recall a single conversation with a girl my age that lasted more than ten seconds. I'm shy, I guess. And because of that I had become an expert at pretending girls didn't matter.

Except over the summer there was someone who liked me, a girl in our sister cabin. Now, as I hit the RBG (that's what we called Ruth Bader Ginsberg) mainyard, there she is.

"Hey, Jackson!"

Florence Landesman—nice enough as far as it goes, just not my type. And if you're thinking it's her looks, you're wrong. She's pretty. Maybe even very. No, the trouble with Florence has to do with her general strangeness. I like smart girls who are into science but there are limits. I mean, she spent one of our cabin nights telling me how she likes to catch flies in puddles of shampoo then pull off their wings.

"Oh, hey, Florence," I say. "How you doing?"

"Okay," she says. Then adds nervously. "Going to the dance?"

Mateo shoots me a smile, then waves to Patti who is every bit as pretty as Florence is weird. I mean, of course I'm going to the dance—*everyone* in camp has to go, right? But before I can answer, up strides another major player in the story. You might say he's my archrival, the cabin jerk. In a way, Oliver Kemp isn't all bad—just an overly aggressive, loudmouth in the way that some kids who are good at sports live in the Universe. I have to admit it. Even though Oliver is the shortest kid in our age group, he can hit the living stuffing out of a ball. And if you aren't there to see him do it you're certain to hear all about it because he'll make sure to tell you.

"Sure, Jackson is going to the dance," Oliver calls out, clapping me on the back. "And guess what Florence? He wants to dance with you."

Florence? She lights up like a stoned lightning bug. If I didn't find her so weird, I might have been flattered.

"Really?" Florence says.

"Absolutely," Oliver replies.

"Okay then," she stammers. "Cool." Then to me: "See you inside, okay? Inside the lodge?"

"Sure," I say. "The lodge."

With that, she sort of half runs, half skips, half stumbles away. The minute her back is turned, I take the opportunity to sock Oliver in the shoulder. Hard.

"Why'd you say that?"

He socks me right back—harder. It hurts. I told you, he's small, but strong. The kid has actual muscles.

"Because your need for a girl is obvious."

"I'm fine. I don't need a girl."

Oliver laughs. "Says the kid who sucks face with horses."

Even Mateo has to chuckle at that.

"I don't suck face with horses." I'm going under fast, gasping for air. "What's the big deal anyway? People kiss pets all the time."

"True enough," Oliver says, sauntering now toward the lodge. "But Florence has nicer lips. You won't need to pick her hooves either."

As Oliver Kemp insults go it's pretty harmless. But I guess I'm sick of the whole horse-Jackson-slobber-kiss motif. I have to say something, right? A few weeks earlier, Oliver and the assistant director's daughter, Luna Hart, had hung for a couple of dances then made a date to meet one night at the giant oak tree in the pasture. But she had been a no show. Ghosted him. Now seems like the time to use it.

"Speaking of hooves?" I call. "How were Luna's that night at the oak tree?"

"Is that the best you can do?" Oliver says, wheeling back around. "Luna Hart? She's ancient history."

"Ancient history?" I say. "It was only two weeks ago!"

"Three weeks," Oliver says. "Which is a lifetime at camp." He nods toward the lodge. "I'm moving on, okay? Other horses in the stable."

To that little witticism, he grins big—for a jerk the guy has confidence, I have to give him that—then disappears into the fray.

"Idiot," I mutter.

Mateo drapes an arm around my shoulder.

"True," he says. "But he does have a point. Florence is way into you."

"Maybe," I say. "Just wish I was into her."

Which is when Patti grabs my hand. "Forget Florence," she says yanking me toward the lodge. "Time to find you someone else."

Chapter 3

Who would guess that "someone else" would be Luna Hart?

Moments later, I'm inside the RBG main lodge, a large room that doubles as their dining hall. The tables have been pushed to the sides and a few streamers hung across the ceiling with a sign saying, "DANCE." I stick close to Mateo and Patti, doing my best to avoid Florence, which really isn't all that hard because the place is jammed.

All the other camp dances that summer have gone like this: we Flying Eaglers have gathered on one side of the RBG lodge with the girls on the other. Then after the usual chatter, whoops and giggles, the music started and some counselors got things rolling, dancing with each other, urging the campers to join in. Before long, kids were dancing, too, mostly in big clumps, usually not with anyone in particular. And since I was shy that was fine with me.

But the night of this final dance of the summer, the counselors decide to mix things up. The minute we get inside the lodge we're divided up, boys in one circle, girls in a second, inner circle.

"Okay, people!" one of the counselor's shouts. She's tall, freckled and wears matching a RGB sweatshirt and sweatpants. "Boys walk left, girls walk right!"

I swallow hard. While my twelve-year-old-boyness renders me mostly clueless, it doesn't mean that I'm completely out of touch with reality. The counselors had gotten sick of getting the ball rolling themselves every week. Now they're trying something different, matching us up, one-on-one.

"Yo, Jackson! Walk, bro!"

That's Mateo, of course. But with the circles beginning to move, I have a crazy idea that there's still time to sneak out of the lodge and escape back to Flying Eagle, raid the kitchen, then crawl into my sleeping bag with a book and a few pouches of hot cocoa mix. (I like to eat 'em raw). Anything other than to be forced into a cringe-worthy conversation with someone I don't know. Or worse, the booby prize: Florence. I don't think I could bear another conversation about fly-dissection.

"Jackson," Mateo says. "Move it!"

This time it comes with a shove. Next thing I know I'm on a merry-go-round from which there's no escape, going round and round clockwise, with the circle of girls walking the other way. Tall girls, short girls, older, younger, thin, heavy, pretty, prettier, less-pretty, braces, retainers, freckles, glasses, pigtails, lip gloss, blonde, brunette, black, white, Asian, smiling, frowning, and maybe some just as terrified as I am. Each time I pass Florence I try to look through her without being mean. Then just like that the music stops.

And there she is: Oliver's almost-girl: Luna.

Maybe you're thinking that I had always thought she was

pretty, that she had one of those gleaming toothpaste commercial smiles and cascading blonde hair that she washed every night with extra-strength dishwashing liquid. But that's not it. Not that she isn't pretty, because she is. Her dad, Flying Eagle's assistant director, Lou, is white, while her mom, Amanda, the camp's get-everything-done-behind-the-scenes person, is black. The two of them gave Luna light brown skin and eyes and super curly hair. Also, she's on the short side and has a sort of forthright, statuesque nose, and a big smile that shows lots of teeth and more than the standardly acceptable amount of gums, features that aren't particularly attractive on their own but mesh together to form something extra nice. Still, the thing that really gets my attention is her T-shirt. It's bright pink with bold lettering that reads: "Fight the Power." Pretty political for a twelve-year-old but cool by me. Then things get even better. I notice something about her I never have before.

Cowboy boots.

Not only I have stumbled upon a politically minded girl with a big smile, but someone who likes horses.

"Hey, I'm Luna."

"Yeah, I know," I say. "I mean, I'm in Oliver's cabin."

Do I really bring up Luna's ex-sort-of-boyfriend with my very first words? Luckily, Luna finds it amusing.

"Oh, yeah," she says. "*Him.*" Then she smiles. "So is that your name? Should I call you 'Kid in Oliver's cabin?'"

I swallow hard.

"Do me a favor," I say. "Don't."

"What? Oliver's not your best friend?"

I pause. "Let's just say we have a complicated relationship. Anyway, I'm Jackson."

"Hey, Jackson."

"Hey, Luna."

"All right, kiddos!" another counselor calls. "Time to mooooove!"

Luna is a rule-obeyer. Or maybe she really just likes to

dance. Or feels that I've passed some sort of test. Suddenly, she's shaking like she's been plugged in, flinging her arms and legs this way and that, without a trace of weirdness. Me? I'm so blown away by her boots, her dancing, and her general coolness with the moronic way I had brought up Oliver, that I'm dumbstruck.

"Sorry," she says, eventually noticing that her supposed partner is still stationary. "I just really like this song."

I don't know it and I don't like it but I know enough to realize that this isn't the time to get into a debate about pop music.

"Yeah," I stammer. "Me, too."

Apparently, that's all the reassurance she needs. Once again, Luna takes it up to full blast, waving her arms and moving any part of her body that's capable of being moved. And me? The way I see it, I have two choices: either slink out of the lodge to start my previously planned raid on the Flying Eagle kitchen or get with the program. But is sneaking off really an option? It's gutless for a start, not to mention rude. Also, the assistant cook is probably still on duty. Which leaves dancing. I'm embarrassed to admit, but I actually glance around the lodge for Oliver. Yeah, he had called Luna ancient history. But maybe he's jealous. Maybe he's hiding behind the RBG kitchen counter, ready to pounce like a jungle cat, bite my carotid artery and leave me for the vultures? Then again, maybe not. Wherever he is and whoever he's with, I can't find him.

"Come on!" Luna says.

Then through a tangle of dance-swept hair, she smiles. That's the final push I need—or maybe I'm just too embarrassed to keep standing there doing nothing because I jump off the ledge, fling my limbs this way and that, moving any way I can, praying it all has some slight relation to the beat. I don't ever want to see a vid of whatever it is I'm doing, but I guess it works well enough. Before I know it, the song has ended. Luna and I meet eyes, winded and happy.

One Last Ride

I guess I've passed some sort of a test because when the next song comes on, cranked loud, and other couples begin to split up—I see Mateo and Patti find each other—Luna doesn't head back to the girls' side of the lodge.

"Where you from?" she shouts over the music.

"New York," I call back. "The city."

One thing I've discovered: people who aren't from New York tend to think that living there is a cool thing.

"Nice," Luna says. "I love New York."

"Oh, you've been there?"

She shakes her head. "No, but I've watched the Tonys." She pauses. "I guess that sounds stupid."

"No, that's exactly what New York is like," I say. "Lots of theater people, singing and dancing and accepting awards. They give 'em out on the subway."

Luna laughs. "Maybe I can get one then?"

"For sure. I've got like twenty."

That gets me a smile. With that basic information exchanged, we begin to dance again. Now that the conversation is going, Luna leans close so we can communicate without yelling. It turns out that we're both going into seventh grade. She's in a cabin called Shrewsberry. I'm in Cabin Three. She likes spaghetti best for dinner. I like the Welsh Rarebit. Both camps get donuts on Thursdays. Both camps have a cow, but Flying Eagle's has this rare udder disease that makes her milk undrinkable. On the other hand, Flying Eagle has a working kiln while RBG's is currently out of operation due to an explosion that blew up pieces of camper pottery, but fortunately no actual campers. Then things get interesting.

"What do you like to do here anyway?" she asks. "What activities?"

I glance again at her boots.

"Same as you, I think. Riding."

Luna laughs. "Riding? A New York kid?"

"Yeah."

"There aren't horses in New York."

Actually, there are a few in Central Park—cops ride them—but I let it pass.

"I learned here."

"Just this summer?"

"Yeah."

"You can't be very good then."

She's smiling.

"I suck," I say, playing along. "I can barely stay on. You any good?"

"I live in Maine. They give out riding awards just for being born there."

Now it's my turn to smile. The next half an hour rush by in a blur of shouted conversation, wild dancing, bug juice, more dancing, more shouting, and bathroom breaks. Then we go to the tetherball court where Luna gives me a hard time for not knowing how to do rope tricks, then kicks my butt three out of five. Losing to a girl? Doesn't bother me a bit. I'm having too much fun to care. To tell the truth, I might have dropped the last game because of a slight focus issue. Yeah, Luna and I are playing tetherball in Vermont. But my overly active imagination has us getting married at home plate during the seventh inning stretch of a Mets Game. Officiated by Lin Manuel Miranda. Why not? Luna watches the Tonys, right? I snap back to the now just in time to hear the director of the girl's camp, Mrs. Davenport, a sixty-something Vermonter in a RBG sweatshirt, shorts, and hiking boots, cry out from the steps of the lodge: "Last dance!"

"You wanna?" I ask.

Luna whacks the tetherball a final time with her fist. Then she does something amazing:

She takes my hand!

I'll repeat that, okay?

Luna Hart TAKES MY HAND!

Chapter 4

The perfect end to the perfect evening, right? My first hand-hold on the way to a final dance with a girl. And not with just any girl—a t-shirt-wearing, cowboy-booted, rope trick-executing female who likes to give me a hard time—a girl I can talk to as easily as any guy.

Like I said, perfect.

Unfortunately, I'm about to be sideswiped. We both are, Luna and me. The very instant we set foot in the lodge ready to let loose, the fast and rhythmic music that Luna and I have heard outdoors turns on a dime to a tune with the basic beat of a funeral march. In a blink, Luna looks like she wants to melt into an oil slick. It's hard to blame her. A moment earlier we had been chatting, laughing, playing tetherball—innocent stuff. Suddenly, we're in a mass of hugging teens, a slow-dancing monster sucking us into its void. Don't get me wrong, I want to be sucked in—desperately. Holding a girl like Luna, someone I actually like? That's something I want a part of. Maybe she does, too.

"This is weird, right?" Luna finally manages.

Then she laughs, the last laugh of the doomed.

If you can believe it, at that precise moment, I look for Oliver—anything to give me an excuse to back out. But to my amazement, he's slow-dancing himself! Not only that, but with a girl a full head taller than he is! I look for Luna's dad, but realize that he's probably back at Flying Eagle, planning the next day's activities. There's nothing and no one stopping me—only myself.

I'd like to report that that's the moment when I looked deep within my soul and found the guts to make a move all on my own. But that wouldn't be truth. As more and more kids pair up, I see that Mateo and Patti have also made the leap, becoming one person with four arms, swaying on the wooden floor. Still, my bud manages to catch my eye and motion wildly in Luna's general direction. His meaning can't be clearer: get cracking or take a lifelong membership in the league of losers.

By that time, Luna and I are the only couple in the whole entire lodge that aren't touching—at least that's how it feels.

"So...?" I begin.

Luna moves to her left just in time to avoid a swaying couple. She meets my eyes. I swallow hard.

"You wanna?" I ask.

She answers by taking a single step toward me. I return the favor and somehow we manage to place our dangling arms around each other. If that isn't enough, Luna throws in a final touch: pulling close, she lays her head on my shoulder, wasting me with this earth-shattering whiff of hair. For a second or two we just stand there, stunned stupid by what we've done. Then finally, we begin to sway.

"Wow," she says. "This is a nice surprise."

Holding Luna, a crazy thought crosses my mind. If a simple

slow dance can make a person feel this good, why should it be so hard for a couple to get along? Couldn't my folks take a cue from Luna and me and just hug it out? Wouldn't that take care of my mother's tears? Make my dad feel better, too? "Relationships can be complicated." That's what dad had said, right? But come on! This boy-girl stuff isn't so hard! I have it so covered.

I pull Luna closer and hold tight.

Chapter 5

At the final bell, Mateo and I whoop and holler and brag all the way back to the camp gate. Slow-dancing is nice as far as it goes, sure, but passing into the Flying Eagle pine forest, Mateo lets it be known that he and Patti had gone even further. Namely, they had made out behind the girl's lodge—this time for a full five and a half minutes! You heard me: FIVE AND A HALF MINUTES! It's like their lips had been attached since the Big Bang. Sure, Mateo tries to be modest about it, but is there any truly modest way to announce to a friend that you've made out when he hasn't? In response, I pretend that he's full of it before caving and giving him credit.

"Nice, bro," I say.

Even though it isn't really dark yet, a firefly lights up in front of us then disappears, warming up for nighttime.

"Thanks," Mateo says. "But hey! You and Luna?"

I can't deny it, right? Mateo smiles big and slaps my back. He's genuinely happy for me, you can tell.

"Felt good, right?"

"Yeah, it felt good. Sure it did," I say. Then I can't resist. "You don't think Oliver'll mind?"

"The hell with Oliver," Mateo says. "He found someone else, right?"

"I know. Who was that tall girl?"

"Emma Schivner. I think she's fourteen."

"Wow!"

"I know."

"How about Luna's dad? He wasn't there, right?"

My friend tells me what I already know.

"Lou's back at Flying Eagle and he wouldn't give a hoot anyway." His third summer at camp, Mateo knows things. "You've got to focus on what's next."

"Next?"

Mateo gives me a friendly shove. I know what that means. It's a logical progression, right? I'd be lying if I said that the thought of a kiss hasn't crossed my mind. I'm twelve and a half, after all—it's pretty much time or close enough anyway. But I'd also be lying if I said that I felt confident about my ability to deliver. The only females I've kissed in my life are family relations, lip to cheek. Lip to lip with an actual girl seems miles above my level—especially with the assistant director's daughter.

"Hey," I say. "Luna and I just met."

Mateo drapes an arm around my shoulder. He does that sometimes, too—it's part of his cool thing, along with the purple streaks.

"No one said you had to get married."

Another dose of Mateo non-logic. Had I ever told him I was worried that a kiss might lead to a proposal?

"This was the last dance of the summer," I say. "I may not

even see her again."

A lie and I know it.

"Bull," Mateo says. "You'll see her around this week. And if you don't, there's always the last night of camp at the fair."

The fair, the final activity of the summer where each cabin in both camps throws together some sort of booth. I *had* been looking forward to it.

"So okay," I admit. "I'll see her at the fair."

To tell the truth, that's exactly how Luna and I had said goodbye: "See you at the fair."

"Kiss her there," Mateo says.

"There isn't a kissing booth or something?"

"Kissing booth?" Mateo shakes his head. "Not last year anyway."

A relief. For a second I think I've been trapped.

"Okay, so where would I kiss her then?" I say, back on the offensive. "Out in public by the mainhouse?"

"Why not?"

"Why not?" I say. "Because everyone will see! Her father and mother might see!"

"Who cares?"

"I care! I'm twelve."

"So am I!"

I laugh. "You're almost thirteen and you act like you're fourteen and a half."

Mateo flings an arm around my shoulder again and lowers his voice, like he's passing along privileged info. "Listen, I understand your privacy concerns. That's why the Cabin 8 and 9 kids set up a hang out room."

"A hang out room?" I say. "At the fair?"

"Yeah, where kids can dance. It's excellent."

"So what? I kiss her on the dance floor? That's not private."

"Not *on* the dance floor, you idiot. Last year they had this table and kids went underneath it."

"*Underneath*? Why?"

"Because that's where it's private, get it?"

"But people can see underneath tables!"

Mateo sighs. He's close to giving up on me, a summer project gone wrong. "They drape a blanket over the side, okay? Then you crawl under. They've got pillows in there. Blankets, too, so you can lie down."

"Lie down?" My voice cracks—it had begun to do that. Yes, I had slow-danced, but suddenly Mateo is pushing me into a situation that a nerdy high school senior might find nerve-wracking.

"Yeah, lie down," Mateo says. "That's all. You don't have to take your clothes off. Just go under there and fool around, no big deal."

It isn't high on the standard macho-guy list to admit, but I'm just not ready. Luna and I had just met. Kissing can wait.

"Just think about it this way," Mateo goes on. Now he grins more broadly. "It can't be much different than making out with your horse."

That again?

But the timing is perfect. Before I have time to defend myself yet again, a loud whinny splits the air, followed by a flurry of hooves. Horses on the move. Not trotting or even cantering, but really kicking up dirt, galloping.

"What the heck is that?" Mateo asks.

"Come on," I say.

Mateo and I sprint up the rest of the pine forest path to where it meets the open heart of the Flying Eagle pasture. The sky is streaked orange now and the color bleeds into the meadow where we see Major and Copper running flat out across the upper ballfield, moving quickly toward a path into the pine forest.

"Whoa," Mateo shouts. "It is ON!"

I'm not all that surprised. The two fastest in the stable, Major and Copper are both hard to handle on the trail, itching to air it out on back country roads and prove once and for all who is the best. I have a summer-long suspicion that they're trying to prove themselves to Merrylegs. Whether in the

One Last Ride

pasture or in the riding ring, the two horses vie for position by her side like she's the "it" girl in the school cafeteria.

Now Major and Copper streak up the pasture toward the pine forest almost as though they've slapped hooves over an agreed upon route. Merrylegs doesn't seem to like it. After galloping for a few steps after her two guys, she draws to a sudden halt and neighs loud. That's when Gidget, a tall brown and white pinto and the oldest horse in the stable, canters to her side. "Relax," he seems to be saying. "Let the young bucks have their fun." As for the other horses? While the big white bay, Blondie, watches with half interest, Echo and Strawberry continue to graze, mouths full of grass, as though they find the entire stupid thing a crazy waste of time. That isn't a surprise: they *hate* to run.

As for the race, Copper holds the early lead, tearing though the uncut outfield to the pasture beyond, then into the pine forest. I know the path they're taking—it snakes through the thick woods and comes out just below where Mateo and I are standing. Peering through the trees we're able to catch glimpses of them, pounding toward us. As the path narrows, Major is forced to duck under branches, which allows the smaller Copper to push his lead.

"Yo, here they come!" Mateo calls.

"Move it!" I yell.

We leap out of the way just as the two horses burst out of the forest, kicking dirt and grass into our faces, stretching toward the lower pasture. Yes, Major has fallen further behind, but back out in the open, he's able to extend those long legs and make up ground. With a wide right around a giant oak it's a straight shot now, up a grassy incline to where Merrylegs and the other four horses are waiting by home plate, now joined by Trudi, the camp cow.

By then a crowd of Flying Eagle kids, all returning from RBG, are screaming. It's pretty funny. Since only a small percentage go to the ranch, most of them don't even know the name of the horse they're rooting for.

"Move your butt, ya fat beast!"

"Go, go, go!"

With no more than thirty feet to go, Copper is still ahead but tiring fast. Soon, Major has cut the lead to a length. Then a half! But then Copper bursts across home plate a fraction of a second ahead. Both horses pull up immediately, dripping sweat, fried to the max. Copper is the victor, sure enough, but if he's been hoping to win over Merrylegs with speed, it doesn't seem to have worked. She nuzzles Major first.

That's when Doug, Mateo and my counselor and ranch head, comes up from behind. He's twenty-one and has sandy blonde hair with gentle features to match a gentle demeanor—a nice guy all around.

"This is what happens when we don't take an afternoon trail ride."

"You think?" I ask.

Doug nods. "They needed to burn off some steam, that's all."

"They sure did," Mateo says.

I still think the race has more to do with a summer-long rivalry between the two horses over Merrylegs than the sudden need for some evening exercise.

"You two had fun at the dance," Doug goes on. "That's how it looked anyway."

Mateo shrugs, a man of the world, while I stammer like a maniac and blush brighter than one of the fireflies. As for Doug, he picks at a piece of timothy and doesn't say another word. He's good that way, nice enough to know that I'd want that slow-dance recognized, but considerate enough to understand that I don't want to be pushed to the point of an actual discussion. Our other counselor, Rusty, isn't so subtle.

"Yo!" he calls, trotting up to my side. "Lou's daughter! She's a nice girl, kid! Smart, too, I hear."

Where Doug wears his gentleness on his sleeve, Rusty sports this out-going hippy-rebel vibe—dark hair to his shoulders and sideburns that the girls of RBG seem to like. So far that summer, he's had two girlfriends—and those were the ones I knew about.

"You really like her?" I ask.

"Absolutely," Rusty says, rubbing a large hand through my hair. "Nice going."

By that point, the last streaks of orange are fading from the sky and the first distant stars are glimmering. As the horses become outlines in the near dark, Mateo, Doug, Rusty and I make our way up the dirt road that leads out of the pasture, past the small farm to the Flying Eagle main yard. As we cut down to the cabins—an area called "the row"—I notice a quarter moon hanging there in the sky. A sweet sight to mark the end of a sweet night.

"All right, boys," Doug calls. "Brush teeth and then to bed."

Chapter 6

Any camp cabin features a unique cast of characters. Along with Oliver, the self centered athlete, Mateo, the cool pretty-boy insider, and me, the blend into the scenery city kid who had gotten lucky with a slowdance, there are two other guys who round out our little band in Cabin Three.

First is Noah Ollinger. A little bit on the, well, heavy side (I know it's uncool to say it), he sleeps on the bunk above me. Super out-going, Noah is a slob who cruises around camp in three interchangeable pairs of high tops, one orange, one black, one red. On the first night of the summer he announced something interesting at dinner. "Yo, everyone," he said. "Just to be clear, I might be gay though I'm currently inactive." Being boys of the 21st Century, we took it in stride. Maybe he was and maybe he wasn't. Probably he just doesn't know yet. Who really cares? Noah's a fun guy, as long as you didn't mind a near constant stream of comments, questions, and bad advice.

Then there's Garth Wells. As quiet as Noah's loud, he's a dark-haired boy from down south somewhere—I think Nashville—with blue rimmed glasses who had arrived at camp with a knapsack full of books, everything from scientific texts to histories of foreign lands to an annotated *Lord of the Rings*. Even though he's straight, old Garth knows even less about girls than Noah or me or really anyone. To his credit, he doesn't seem to care.

Still, even Garth is interested in that night's gossip. Once we've brushed teeth and are in our bunks, Rusty reads us a story and Doug plays his guitar for a few minutes—he's written a few funny songs about Courtney, his girlfriend from college. My favorite is "You Say She's Ugly, but I Say She's Beautiful, What of It?" Anyway, after all that, our two counselors say goodnight and the boy-talk begins.

First up is Oliver. To my relief, he cares less that I've hooked up with Luna.

"Emma is amazing, dudes," he declares from his bunk—he sleeps on the far side of the front door, above Doug. "One for the record books."

"Is she really fourteen?" Mateo asks from his upper bunk above Rusty.

"Better. Fourteen *and a half*."

To that, we nod. I mean, it *is* an impressive number.

"She's the lead in the musical, too," Oliver goes on. "Cool, right?"

Flying Eagle and RBG are putting on a production of *In The Heights*, a show about a Hispanic community in uptown New York City—a weird choice considering there are maybe a total of three Latinos in both camps.

"That is cool," Noah says. "But come on. Let's be real."

"Be real?" Oliver replies. "What do you mean?"

One Last Ride

"She's like a foot taller than you, bro. You look like her little brother."

Leave it to Noah to verbalize what we are all thinking. But Oliver isn't insulted.

"Don't you morons see?" he says. "The height difference is what makes it so good!"

"Why?" Garth asks.

"My head fits perfectly in the nook in between her chest!"

Our hoots and hollers nearly blow the roof off the cabin.

"The old head on the chest trick," Mateo says, as if taking notes for future use. "I like it."

I expect Oliver to go off some more about Emma's chest, maybe even describing how it felt, but Noah is already leaning his head over his bunk to mine.

"What about Luna?" he asks. "Did you two slowdance, too? Or were my eyes playing tricks?"

"No tricks," I say, proudly. "We slowdanced, all right."

Leave it to Noah. He turns right to Oliver.

"And you're okay with this? Your ex-girl with Jackson?"

If I had been worried that Oliver would throw a fit (which I was) I was wrong.

"It's fine with me," he says. "Jackson can have her."

"Jackson can *have her*?" Noah says. "You don't own her, dude."

"Oh, I know," Oliver says. "I'm just saying that I've moved way on."

Fair enough. Luna had ghosted him, right? Anyway, Noah is still looking for more info from me.

"So how'd you ask her?" he asks. "I mean, to slow dance?"

I try to play it cool. "It just sort of happened."

"Yeah, *right*," Mateo calls from his bunk. "With a little push from me."

"Is that true?" Oliver calls. "You needed help, Jackson? Lame, man."

"Hey, I asked her myself...it just took me a little while."

"So what did you say?" Noah says, still leaning down over

me.

"I don't know. I just said, 'you wanna?'"

"That's all it takes?" Garth asks from his bunk on the opposite wall. "You wanna?"

Like I say, he likes books more than girls, but I suppose he's collecting data for future use.

"Yeah," I say, enjoying my new found status as 'a guy who knows things.' "That's it."

"And she said yes?" Oliver asks.

"To be honest she didn't say anything," I say. "She just sort of spread her arms."

"Nice," Noah says. He slaps me five then looks to the cabin with a wide gap-toothed smile. Along with needing to lose some weight, he also needs braces. "Hear that, dudes? She spread her arms? So what happened then?"

"We just hugged," I say.

"Like with your arms, right?" Garth says.

"No, his feet, idiot!" Oliver calls.

"Yeah, my arms," I say. "Both of 'em!"

I could've relived the moment forever—and I'm about to continue, getting poetic about how it feels to hold a girl that close. But our voices must have still been carrying. Suddenly, the on-duty shines his flashlight into the cabin. I see the silhouette of a lean, muscular frame in the doorway, a man with a mustache—and I shudder. It's Lou, Luna's dad! For a second I think he's come to our cabin to rip me a new one.

"Close it down, guys," he says. "Time to sleep."

"Sorry," Noah says. "Garth was the one doing all the talking anyway."

Lou isn't buying it. "Sorry, Noah. I could hear you all the way up at the Main House."

He doesn't seem angry at anyone, and certainly not at me. Truth to tell, he barely glances my way. Still, part of me half expects him to sit on my bunk and give me a lecture on the evils of underage hugging. Instead, he just says, "Night, boys," and disappears into the darkness.

One Last Ride

I'm relieved, for the moment, anyway. Does Lou know that I had slow-danced with his daughter? If so, he sure isn't saying anything. Anyway, after he leaves, Oliver goes off for a bit more about Emma. Then as exhaustion truly sets in, Noah starts joking that he's kissed someone, too: Garth's grandmother. Garth replies that that's impossible because his grandmom is dead. So Noah says he's kissed Garth's *other* grandmother. Turns out she's dead, too. That finally shuts Noah up, no mean feat and the next thing I know, everyone is quiet. Camp days are long. When sleep comes, it crashes down like ton of bricks.

Chapter 7

We sleep on canvas bunks at Flying Eagle. If that doesn't sound comfortable, it isn't, but I sleep like a log anyway, tucked deep into my sleeping bag with a blanket over me. Tired boys can sleep anywhere, I guess.

Most mornings, I'm out cold straight through to the wake-up bell. But the day after the dance I wake about five minutes early, still psyched. Enjoying the stillness of morning, I glance around the cabin. In keeping with what the camp calls "its pioneer spirit" we aren't allowed cell phones, I-pads, or computers. In fact, there's no electricity in the cabins at all so a lantern is kept on hand to do the job of a light bulb. The other light source is the fireplace. Rusty had started a small blaze the night before, now burned down to a pile of morning ashes.

My cabinmates are all still sprawled out on their bunks. Across the way, glasses off, Garth lays flat on his back, a fallen flashlight by his side, still holding the book on an Introduction to Chemistry he's been reading when he fell asleep. To my right, Rusty snores lightly on the lower bunk. On the upper bunk above him I catch a glimpse of tangled rock-star hair: Mateo. On the other side of the cabin, partially blocked from view by a post, Oliver is stretched out in on the bunk above Doug—like everyone else they are still asleep, too, Doug in a Flying Eagle sweatshirt and Oliver in underwear with no shirt at all. Finally, there's Noah. His large body makes a giant indentation in the canvas above me.

That accounts for the human members of Cabin Three. You might say that we also have a mascot of sorts, a medium-sized chipmunk who lives in a hole by the fireplace and visits now and then throughout the day. Hearing a light pitter patter on the wood floor, I lean on my elbow to watch him come through the front door and rise to his haunches, checking out the scene. His usual visiting hours are after lunch during rest hour—that's when he puts on a show, scurrying around the cabin as we lay on our bunks. That's also when Noah had the brainstorm to name him Harvey Jones, after Flying Eagle's owner and head director. A middle aged man with a slight spread, the real Harvey Jones doesn't look a thing like a chipmunk. But the name sticks anyway.

Anyway, noticing that he's under observation, our little mascot gets up on his haunches again and gives me a look.

"Yo, Harvey," I whisper. "I slow-danced last night."

Unfortunately, the chipmunk doesn't seem to understand the importance of what I'm trying to get across. Still up on his haunches, he looks at me sort of strangely for a moment, then bolts through a crack in the wall.

"Bye, Harvey," I whisper. "See you at rest hour."

Again, the cabin is still. Then the spell is broken by the bright clang-clang of the morning bell, echoing down to the cabins all the way from the top of the main house. Rusty groans. Oliver rolls over and tucks his head under his pillow. Garth stretches, sending his flashlight banging to the floor. As always, Doug is the first to actually sit up.

"All right, everyone," he calls groggily. "Rise and shine."

By that point, Rusty is sitting up, long legs dangling to the floor. As always, he sleeps in a pair of one piece body-length red underwear.

"Yeah, everyone," he groans, doing his part to help. "Come on!"

That's when Mateo makes his appearance, flopping to the floor, landing directly in front of Rusty's trunk in green pajamas. It's always sort fun to see him in the morning. It's the one time of day his hair is a mess. Pillow head.

"Morning, Mateo," Rusty says.

"Morning, Rusty," Mateo replies. "You snored last night."

"Yeah? You drooled on your pillow."

"Not drool," Mateo says matter of factly. "It's where I practice making out."

Seems like a perfectly good use of a pillow. In any case, that's Noah's cue. Flopping out of his bunk, he lands hard in front of me and slips into a pair of jeans and his orange high tops. Then Oliver, shirtless to show off his muscles, I guess, jumps out of his bunk and hops frantically around the cabin.

"Darn, it's cold!" he cries. "Crap! Crap! CRAP!" before finally grabbing a flannel robe from his trunk.

That leaves Garth.

"Up you go, buddy," Rusty says, giving him a light shove.

Garth yawns, reaches for his blue glasses and tucks his book back into his knapsack. Only then does he crawl out of his sleeping bag.

With everyone up, I take the opportunity to share the first news of the day.

"Guess who was here this morning, guys?" I say. "Harvey Jones."

Mateo grins. "You told him about your slow-dance, right?"

He has me dead to rights—one of the problems with having

a friend who knows you too well. But in no galaxy am I admitting to telling a chipmunk about Luna.

"No way," I say.

"What was he up to anyway?" Noah asks. "He didn't pee in one of my high tops, did he?"

"Is your foot wet?" Oliver calls from the other side of the cabin.

"Actually, no. Feels pretty dry in there."

"Then he didn't pee in your frigging high tops."

"All right, guys," Doug says. He's leaning out the front door now. "Looks like a nice day. Let's get ready for it."

And so we rub the sleep from our eyes and file down to the washhouse to brush our teeth. Then we straighten our sleeping bags, sweep the cabin and clean the lantern for inspection. Then comes the second bell of the day.

"All right, guys," Doug calls. "Breakfast!"

Off we go. I don't wear shoes because I like the feel of the grass on my barefeet. By that point in the summer, my soles have become callused to where I can take a direct hit from whatever rock, pebble, or stick the ground has to offer and barely flinch. Anyway, soon we're up at Flying Eagle's mainyard, a large spread of grass marked by three buildings that are so old they were probably built by the first pioneers. Across the way from the yellow main house and dininghall is a two-story barn so ancient it leans. Down by the camp lane stands a little red building called the post office. It leans in the other direction.

"Jackson Segal and Mateo Greene!"

My buddy and I turn around. Up trots Kent Lee, leader of waterfront.

"What?" Mateo asks.

Kent shoves an envelope into Mateo's hands.

"This came while I was down at morning dip."

Mateo and I are stunned. The Pond Express: inotherwords, the way RBG and Flying Eagle kids exchange letters. As in, boy, girl letters!

One Last Ride

"It just came?" Mateo asks.

I mean, it's hard to believe. A letter...*already*?

Kent nods. "That it did. Enjoy, gentlemen."

With a quick smile he leaves Mateo and me to stumble to the side of the main house. To our astonishment, we see our names written on the cover of the envelope in careful cursive.

Mateo Greene and Jackson Segal

"Open it!" I command.

Mateo is already tearing it apart, mangling the envelope beyond recognition.

"Don't rip it," I say, grabbing for the letter.

"Hands off," Mateo says, grabbing it back. "My name's first!"

He throws the envelope to the ground and unfolds the letter so forcefully it almost rips.

"What's it say?" I ask.

I look over Mateo's shoulder and we read together.

Hi Guys,

We had fun last night. Maybe we can see you soon? Let's set it up.

Xo, Patti and Luna

In the history of poetic boy/girl communication, the note isn't much. But to Mateo and me it's as if Taylor Swift has highjacked a military helicopter and flown to Vermont to sing us an aria. But where I'm still in a state of bewildered amazement, Mateo's mind is already reeling.

"This is better than I even thought!"

"I know," I say. "We text them back, ask them to meet somewhere?"

The minute the words are out of my mouth, I want to take them back. As I said, Flying Eagle kids aren't allowed electronics, a rule everyone pretty much obeys. Sure, Mateo has an I-Phone 11 that he charges secretly every day at the darkroom, but he mostly uses it to listen to music with headphones to help him fall asleep.

"This is camp, remember?" Mateo says, telling me what I

already know. "No, we need some stationery and an envelope. Gotta write them back."

"To what? Meet?"

"Of course to meet! They said to set it up."

This is all seeming pretty fast. "Is that okay? I mean, will we get in trouble?"

"Maybe," Mateo says. "But this is the last week of camp. If we can't sneak out now when will we?"

"But Luna stood Oliver up! She ghosted him."

"So what? That was Oliver."

Just then, Doug calls from the door to the main house.

"Mateo! Jackson! Come on! Inside!"

Our love lives have to wait. First things first: food. Growing boys, after all.

Chapter 8

Tables, benches, chairs, pictures of old-time campers on the walls. Also screaming boys. That's what makes up the Flying Eagle dininghall. As Mateo and I make it through a twisted weave of hungry campers to Cabin Three's table, Harvey Jones (the real Harvey Jones, not the chipmunk) waddles to the microphone to say grace. After that short nod to civilization, the room shoots to the decibel level of an average rocket launch. Cereal boxes are gouged open, milk cartons ripped, and orange juice poured. Silverware? What the heck is that? Food is engulfed more than eaten—especially by Noah.

"Not bad," he calls, shoving half a pancake into his mouth.

"That's disgusting, you know that?" Garth says, looking up from a book. He reads during most meals.

"What?" Noah replies, mouth still full. "It's my fault that I require food?"

"No," Oliver says, tossing a piece of bacon into his mouth. "But chew sometimes."

"It is what people do," Mateo says. "Normal people anyway."

Noah isn't convinced. "Waste of time. Look at it this way: If I don't chew, I only have to brush twice a week."

With that, he washes down his pancake with a giant gulp of milk then opens his mouth as wide as it can go, exposing all of his teeth down to the last molar. I know that Noah brushes every night—I've seen him—but given his sickening eating habits, I'm surprised by the whiteness of his enamel. Maybe there really is something to his "no-chew" theory? Anyway, a few insults later, breakfast conversation moves to the usual subjects: baseball, that day's activities, camp gossip. Meanwhile, I lean close to Mateo.

"We're really going to ask them to meet?"

"Yeah. After breakfast when we write back. That's our move."

"For when though?"

"Tonight."

I nearly cough up my Fruit Loops.

"That soon? Shouldn't we wait?"

"What for?" Mateo asks.

Before I can answer, our cabin has an unexpected visitor.

"Well, well, well. How is Cabin Three this morning?"

I know that voice instantly. We all do.

Harvey Jones, the human one. A visit from our director isn't necessarily a bad thing—all things considered he's nice enough, if a bit weird. Along with wearing the same outfit every day—a set of interchangeable yellow polo shirts and plaid shorts—he's prone to strange bouts of tuneless humming. Anyway, given the note Mateo and I have just received from Patti and Luna, I'm shaking.

"Hey, Harvey," I say. "Just eating breakfast. See? Fruit Loops. Not doing anything else. Just eating."

As Mateo kicks me under the table, Harvey smiles at me like I'm insane. Clearly, my social life has nothing to do with his visit. Or does it? Because a short second later, Lou is there, too. Luna's dad! Now I'm panicking. Has he heard about the slow dance? The note? Are the director and his assistant gathering to arrange some sort of punishment? Haul me off to the Cabin One washhouse to dunk my head in the toilet? Attach me to the four-speed tractor then drag me through the pigsty until I confess? Who knows what an angry father and strange camp director are capable of—anything, right?

"I've been thinking," Harvey says to Doug. "We should do it."

Tie me to the top of the barn for the crows to peck to death?

"Let's have a horseshow."

I blink. The horse show? Have I heard correctly?

"All right," Doug says.

"I was thinking Wednesday morning could work," Lou says, looking at a schedule he always carries.

Doug nods agreeably but only because he's pretty much always agreeable. I know from overhearing conversations at the ranch that he and Scott, the other riding counselor, hate the horse show: too much work.

"Wednesday it is," Doug says.

"Good," Harvey says.

"I'll mark it on the calendar," Lou says.

His business finished, Harvey gets up from the table then trots off humming one of his unknowable tunes. Meanwhile, Lou gives us all a quick smile.

"Don't forget. I have you guys down for Wednesday morning's shower announcement."

To make shower days more fun—twice a week of enforced soap—each cabin is responsible for coming up with some sort of goofy sketch. The most well received was when Cabin Nine dragged Trudi the cow into the diningroom and soaped her down with baseball mitts. Ours had been mostly disastrous. The most recent effort featured a solo tap dance by Noah (in his red high tops) as Garth rapped the opening lines of *War and Peace*. What that had to do with showers, no one knew.

"Don't worry," Doug says. "We'll be ready."

"Planning another tap dance?" Lou asks Noah.

Noah shakes his head. "Nah, maybe we'll have Garth give a reading this time about the fall of Carthage."

Garth might have responded...except he's too busy reading about the fall of Carthage.

As Lou saunters away, Mateo leans into me.

"Relax," he whispers to me. "See? Lou doesn't know about last night, okay?"

I force myself to get my act together. I guess Mateo is right. I'm going to live to fight another day. Time to change the subject.

"So?" I say to Doug. "A horse show?"

He sighs and rolls his eyes. "Looks that way."

I know what it entails: a series of events and competitions on the horses, featuring the better riders in camp. That includes me, I assume, but before I can ask, Rusty is calling for us to pass our plates up the table. As he scrapes our leftovers into one bowl, Harvey rises to his feet and rings a set of wind chimes by the head table.

"Okay," he says into a microphone. "Time for announcements. What's happening today at the waterfront?"

An so it goes. Swimming, the farm, woodshop, woodcraft, athletics—Flying Eagle has all the usuals. And riding, of course. That day, Doug calls Group One (beginners) first period and Group Three (me) second period. Once announcements are over everyone storms out of the main house like savages. Mateo and I push and shove even more than usual. After all, we have a date with destiny.

"Stationery and an envelope," Mateo says, once we were

outside. "You got 'em?"

"Sure," I say. "But what're we going to say?"

"Leave that to me," Mateo says "Come on."

He takes off for our cabin at a wild sprint, hair flapping in the morning breeze. I glance around the main yard to make sure Harvey and Lou aren't watching, then follow behind as fast as I can.

> Pond Express
>
> To   Patti Vost
>   and
>   Luna Hart

Chapter 9

Flying Eagle has a free and easy vibe, but according to Mateo, the final week of camp follows a hard and fast schedule. On the last Wednesday of each summer is the big softball game against Camp Holiday Farms. Even though I pretty much stink, I'm on the team—an early summer decision before I found riding. Needless to say, Oliver is the star. Anyway, on Thursday night is the musical, *In the Heights*. Then the last Friday night before Saturday morning pick-up is the famous fair where I'm supposed to kiss Luna. Tonight, Monday, is Camp-Wide Capture the Flag—and that game is the key to Mateo's plan. Before I know it, he's sitting on his trunk huddled over a piece of my stationery. Without consulting me, he pens a quick note then reads it out loud.

Greetings Ladies,

Lovely to receive your charming note! We'd be delighted to see you, too, and tonight's Camp Wide Capture the Flag should make it easy to meet at a convenient location. Can you get away, too? 7:30ish perhaps? We are happy to travel to RBG. Where's the best spot for our meeting?

Sincerely, the boys (Mateo and Jackson)

"What do you think?" Mateo asks.

What do I think? I shake my head. "Lovely to receive your charming note?" "Greetings Ladies?" It sounds as if Mateo has been transported to 19th Century England. Still, I keep my criticism of his fancy prose style to myself. What I can't stay quiet about is the risk involved in the whole crazy stunt, especially given Luna's relation to Flying Eagle's senior staff.

"It can't really be that easy to sneak over to RBG, can it?"

"Sure it is," Mateo says, folding the letter into the envelope. "You know how big this camp is. Everybody'll be all over the place. And don't worry about Lou, either. He'll be at the lodge, planning the fair or something."

"But there are other counselors besides Lou, right? Lots of them. What if we get caught?"

Mateo smiles.

"What?" I say.

"You aren't worried about getting caught. You're freaking about kissing Luna. But you don't have to, okay? There's no pucker police that's going to grab your lips and glue them to hers."

I can't let that go by without some sort of comeback, can I? I mean, protocol calls for it. But sometimes your mind goes blank. Then Mateo added on.

"While you two are talking about the best way to shovel a stall, you're more than welcome to watch Patti and me make out," he says. "Maybe learn something."

"Learn from you?" I shout. "You practice on your pillow!"

Mateo comes right back at me.

"Which is why I'm so frigging good at it!"

There's just no rattling this kid. Mateo writes the names Luna Hart and Patti Vost on the front of the envelope and the words POND EXPRESS underneath.

"I'm going swimming first period," he says. "I'll make sure it gets over to RBG."

I still can't quite believe that a plan of such daring has been put into action so quickly—and without my full approval. Maybe Mateo realizes he's pushed too hard. He gives my shoulder a soft punch.

"The girls may not even be able to meet anyway. We'll just send the letter and see how it plays out."

I nod. The truth is there's no cosmic directive to kiss, right? If things go well maybe Luna and I can recreate our slow-dance and hug it out for a while? And if I get too nervous I can always refuse to go. And who knows? Maybe Luna will pull an Oliver and ghost me?

"Right," I say with a nod. "We'll see how it plays out."

Mateo nods. "Good."

He had gone to breakfast wearing his bathing suit, so he's out the door with a towel (and our letter) in a heartbeat, leaving me alone in the cabin.

While most ranches require actual riding boots to get on a horse, Doug and Scott usually let us get away with sneakers. But long pants are a requirement. Since I'm still in shorts, not to mention barefoot, I need to change. Standing in the middle of the cabin, I slide out of my cut-offs, step into my jeans, then begin to pull them up. But when they're at my knees, I see a shadow by the front door. At first, I assume it's someone from the cabin, maybe Doug coming back to change into long pants, too. Or maybe I had just missed the first activity bell and the counselor in charge of daily inspection is already on the job. As it turns out, there's an even worse case scenario. Jeans at my knees, I find myself face to face with the best-looking woman at Flying Eagle. The fact that Michelle Pleshka is virtually the *only* woman at Flying Eagle doesn't change the fact that she's insanely pretty. Everyone thinks it. Everyone discusses it. Twenty-something with a sweet smile, brown hair and dimples, her general hotness is a given, like the blue sky on a cloudless day or the smell of manure at the ranch. Surprisingly at ease in a camp of crazed guys, I'll bet that every single male of the species, counselor and camper, has imagined at some point that she's his girlfriend. That includes me. I have this recurring fantasy where I go up to Sunrise, her cabin, with a couple of bottles of coke, some cupcakes and a strobe light.

Anyway, as camp nurse Michelle has free reign to go down to the cabins, seeing to bumps and bruises and dispensing morning meds to those in need, but it's a privilege she's careful not to abuse. Which means that seeing her materialize at our door is a shock to my system. Even I know that she hasn't dropped by to see me in my underwear. Has she somehow caught wind of our meeting with the girls and come to chew me out? Does she come bearing bad news from home?

"Michelle!" I say, too loudly. "Hey!"

Before she can reply, disaster hits. In an effort to get my jeans up around my waist as quickly as I can, I trip on my pants leg, lurch forward a step, then somersault dramatically backwards onto my bunk, exposing my underweared rear-end directly to her face. I'm pretty sure she sees my crack. I mean, it's right there.

"Jackson!" Michelle cries. "Are you all right?"

Then she laughs, this full throated giggle that fills the cabin. I scramble to my feet, pulling up my underwear so fast I give myself a wedgy. But then as I reach for my jeans I trip again — this time forward and right into her arms!

"Oh, God," I say.

Michelle laughs again. If I could have died on the spot, I might have gone for it.

"Can I help you?" she asks.

"Pull up my pants? No, I've got it."

Mortified, I fall back onto my bunk and manage to get my

jeans up and snapped without exposing myself further.

"Jeez," Michelle says. "That was quite a tumble!"

She laughs again. This time I laugh along with her. I mean, what else can I do? Scream? Make her pinky swear that she'll never tell anyone? Besides, she's seen guys in their underwear before. The woman *is* a nurse.

Still, I can't figure out why she's there. But then, as I'm finally standing back up, buckling my belt, I see the clipboard in her right hand—a list of every camper in camp. I remember that along with her nursing duties Michelle has been put in charge of keeping track of every camper's end-of-the-summer travel plans.

"I wanted to catch you at breakfast and got too busy," she says. "Harvey needs to know. Are you taking the bus back to New York on Saturday or are your parents picking you up?"

I swallow. At least one parent is coming to get me but I honestly don't know if it'll be both or just one. Michelle looks at me sympathetically. She's one of the only people at Flying Eagle who knows the real reason behind the decision to send me here. And that isn't because my folks warned her ahead of time to keep an eye out for me. No, I've only myself to blame. To my total and complete shame I had blurted out what was happening at home to her three weeks earlier—not calmly either, but blubbering like an infant, crying so hard it was hard to speak.

It had happened on Visiting Day. I had known my parents were coming up together—my mom had written me that much. But as the date approached I had gotten more and more stressed. How would they behave? Would they fight? Wrestle to the death in front of the woodshop? Tell me they were divorcing then make me draw-up the settlement right there in the main yard? I was so terrified that the moment I saw our old Ford, a wreck of a city car if there ever was one, pull into the main yard I wanted to run for it—maybe hide out in the washhouse (even the bravest adult wouldn't dare go there, right?) until they got frustrated and left. But once I saw my folks smile my way, I relaxed. I hadn't been homesick all summer—not for a single second—but to my surprise I was even happier to see them than I thought I'd be. We rushed into each others' arms, held there for a good ten seconds, then talked, falling into our old rhythms, a family again. I showed them around camp—our cabin, the pond, the pasture, everything. Dad smiled a lot, something he hadn't done much in the past year. Mom seemed relaxed. When Doug let me ride Merrylegs at the ranch, I let my mind go to a dangerous place. "Alone time" had done its job! Yes! Weren't my parents applauding me as I rode around the ring? Weren't they beaming as I dismounted and led Merrylegs back to the hitching post? Didn't I see my father briefly take my mom's hand? By the time I had taken off Merrylegs' saddle and brushed her down, I practically expected my parents to renew their vows on the roof of the barn while the entire camp cheered.

Too bad that real life intruded. There wasn't an argument—my parents never really argued. I didn't hear a single negative word that might have caused the shift in mood either. But by the time we were walking the short dirt road from the ranch to the main yard there was a tension in the Vermont air that I hadn't felt since I had I left New York. My dad sighed only once, but sometimes a single sigh can say everything, right? My mother tried to cover over whatever was bothering her with cheerful observations. "What a camp!" she'd say. Then she'd repeat it, but with an edge: "What a beautiful camp! Jackson! Look at the size of that magnificent pig!" By the time we got to their car I could bet that any words exchanged between them on the long ride back to the city wouldn't be wedding vows. I had never seen my mom look so sad. I wondered if they would talk at all.

I had held it all in until the following afternoon. I was grateful that when Michelle asked me about visiting day we were near enough to her cabin so that when the tears came she was able to hustle me inside, away from public view. I'm

One Last Ride

also grateful for how she listened and passed me Kleenex, one by one, while I blubbered like a brain-damaged idiot. Once I had calmed down, she said all the right things, too. Like that I had no idea what was going to happen, good or bad, when I got home. And even if my parents did divorce, they both loved me. That would never change. In time, she patched me up enough to ship me back to my cabin for dinner. I never told another soul about what happened or exchanged another word with Michelle about it either. But it was always there, in the air, whenever we said hi or met eyes.

Now, standing at my cabin door, watching me tie my sneakers, I know why she's trekked down to my cabin to ask me when no one else is around—to spare my feelings in case I have another nervous breakdown. Thankfully, I hold it together.

"Someone's coming," I say. "I'm not sure who yet."

I can tell my voice is shaking.

"I'll put down that you're getting picked up then," she says. Then she smiles, gently. "I can get you permission to call home or email to find out."

That's actually a pretty big deal. I think Flying Eagle has a couple of land lines—that's it. Of course, part of me wants to find out who's coming to get me. But I don't want to act like I care too much. To tell the truth, I'm also a little bit paranoid. What if neither of them are coming? What if they tell me then and there on the phone that they're splitting and shipping me off to a convent in Peru?

"Nah, that's okay."

"You sure?"

I nod.

"All right," Michelle says. "If you need to talk, you find me. Just between you and me."

"Yeah, thanks."

She leaves. As I watch her walk back up to the main yard, I sooth my spirits by briefly imagining Michelle feeding me grapes in some fancy restaurant. But once she's disappeared past Cabin One to the main yard, the gloomier thoughts come. Who really *is* picking me up anyway? How are my parents really doing? Are they fighting non-stop? Or are they getting along? Feeding each other heaping plates of spaghetti while painting each other's toenails? Their letters have been cheerful, sure, but a big fat nothing in terms of where they stand. Back on my bunk, I feel a darkness settle over me. There are times that I wish that I hadn't caught my mother crying, looking so upset. Why had they been so open with me about their problems? Wouldn't it have been better to have lied, told me that everything was fine, so I could enjoy the summer without wondering how everything would turn out?

"Hey! Is that you, Jackson?"

This time I know it: I really have missed the first activity period bell. Jay Kriegel, that day's inspector and head of Weavery, stands at the door. If he reports me my cabin will receive a demerit, a mini tragedy that might mean a smaller pot of treats for me and my bunkmates the final night of camp.

"Yeah," I say quickly. "But you didn't see me, okay?"

Jay smiles. "See what?"

I sigh. Thank God for small favors—I need one.

"Thanks."

I duck past Jay and get out of there. It's riding for groups one and three. I don't want to miss out.

Chapter 10

Running late, I sprint all the way through the main yard then up the dirt road that leads to the pasture. By the time I round the corner to the ranch, Flying Eagle's seven horses are already being saddled. Dark coated Major and the pinto Copper have claimed their usual spots at the first hitching post on either side of the ever desirable Merrylegs, while Gidget, Blondie, Strawberry, and Echo graze lightly at the second. With Group One riding, Doug and Scott put me right to work, first helping a younger camper pull the girth strap under Copper, then picking Blondie and Echo's hooves. After that, I help lead the horses to the center of the ring.

Major is in an especially foul mood, probably still angry after losing the race to Copper—at least that's what I think. I hope Doug and Scott don't make me ride him. To tell the truth, I've only been on Major's back twice all summer, both times so terrified I could barely function. While nothing had gone wrong, we had both known that he could've bucked me all the way to Pakistan if he'd wanted. Worse, he could've galloped, the ranch's most serious sin. Ten years earlier a horse named Caramel had run around the ring—really taken off—then tripped and broken his leg so badly that he had to be put down. No one wants to see something like that happen again.

So while Group One takes their turns, Major is given a break. As for me, I spend the time lounging in the middle of the ring, praying that when it's my chance to ride that I get Merrylegs or Echo, one of the gentler horses. With Group Three called for second period, I'm determined to prove myself. I'm worried that I've been promoted before I deserve it, pushed up the ranks not due to my skill but because Doug likes me. A week earlier I had been invited to join in an evening of pasture horseback tag, a game which is played pretty much exactly the way it sounds. While Doug and Scott and the other kids whooped and galloped, I could barely get my horse to move. Partly it was because I was stuck with Blondie, a stubborn beast who sweated like she had just spent an entire day on the cross trainer. Despite a solid hour of kicks and threats, she refused to give me more than one lousy canter—and that only around the ballfield. Scott and Doug were good-natured afterwards—they were always nice—but I knew I had failed, in Scott's eyes anyway. I had good form, especially for someone who had just started, but I rode scared.

My ultimate test is coming. When the Group One kids scurry to their next activity, I look toward the pasture gate. Perfectly on cue, the other boys of Group Three round the corner, side by side, with a swagger that reminds me of a posse from one of those old-time westerns. To the left, and the tallest, a lean five foot ten or so, is Scott's younger brother, Greg. Fifteen years old and the best rider in camp by a longshot, Greg is a perfectly polite kid who rides with perfect form. In the middle is another lanky older boy and one of the only African American kids in a camp of mostly white guys. He's Barry Pepper and, like Greg, he is essentially nice and comfortable atop pretty much any horse. Finally, there's Joey Ambrose, a long-haired, thirteen-year-old who grew up in Vermont riding Western Saddles. Wild on a horse and wild off it, Joey can be likable when he's in the mood but more often steers his Grand Canyon sized ego in the direction of being a jerk.

"Hey, Jackson," Barry calls as they approach. "So it's true? You're in Group Three now? Nice!"

I'm not particularly good at reading between the lines. Is Barry congratulating me or saying that I don't deserve to be there? Maybe a bit of both.

"Yeah," I call back. "I am. Thanks."

Now Greg chimes in.

"Good for you, bro. Congrats."

I take his congratulations at face value. As the best rider in camp what does Greg care if some stupid twelve-year-old has been promoted, even undeservedly, to his group? He's too busy being good at things to care about much else.

"Thanks, Greg," I say.

That leaves Joey.

"What a joke," he says. "If you couldn't get Blondie out of the infield during tag what makes you think you can ride with us now?"

I know that my only hope at emerging with my pride intact is to give it right back to him.

"Yo, that was one night," I say. "I deserve to be here."

What else can I say? That he's right? That I'm terrified? That I suck? That I'm Doug's pet? That I'm unworthy of living?

Joey simply laughs. Luckily, he has a more pressing concern than me on his mind: which horse he'll get to ride.

"Yo, Scott," he calls to the ring. "Copper today?"

His usual choice. Copper is strong and fast, and Joey rides him well. But Scott wants to mix things up.

"Nope," Scott calls back. "Let's give Copper to Jackson."

I breath in sharply. Copper is an easier ride than Major but still treacherous, fast, and hard to control when he's in a bad mood.

"Aw, come on!" Joey says.

Scott ignores him—a typical tactic when dealing with Joey Ambrose—and lets Doug assign the rest of the horses.

"Barry, you give Major a try. Greg, take Merrylegs. Joey, you grab Strawberry."

Joey blinks.

"Strawberry?" He looks like he had just been offered a plate of chipped beef for dessert. "That sack of crap?"

Doug smiles, ever calm. "We don't say sack of crap around here, Joey. We say sack of manure."

"Sack of manure then."

Scott weighs in. "Strawberry's a nice horse, but you can take Blondie instead."

Joey shakes himself: the Universe was conspiring against him. "Blondie? She's the sweatiest animal in human history!"

"Strawberry or Blondie," Scott says. "Those are your choices. Or maybe you want to shovel stalls?"

"*Stalls?*"

Joey practically pukes on the word. Then without missing a beat, he jumps onto the hitching post, stands there perfectly balanced in his cowboy boots, then cups his hands to his mouth: "Hear this, one and all!" he shouts. "That means you Harvey Jones! Doug Gartner and Scott Hill are mistreating a FULL PAYING camper! You hear that? FULL PAYING! This is tyranny!"

I laugh—we all do. Even Joey smiles as he jumps back to the ground. To be fair, he has a certain rough charm. And in this case, he truly has gotten the raw end of the deal: a choice between two lousy horses or a morning with a shovel. Even so, he caves. "Sweaty" beats out "sack of crap." He takes Blondie.

Soon enough we're mounted up.

"Listen up," Doug says, as we settle in the center of the

One Last Ride

ring. "Scott and I have hashed it out. There's going to be a horseshow this Wednesday morning. You four are going to be in the advanced walk, trot, canter."

Given my promotion to Group Three I guess it makes sense, but I'm still flattered to be included. That said, everyone knows that if there's a contest, Greg is going to win.

"Okay," Scott says. "Let's get walking around the ring. Barry: Take the lead."

Now it's his turn to be surprised.

"What? On *Major*?"

Scott smiles. "See how it goes."

Apparently, I'm not the only one getting tested.

Barry's hands are shaking—I can see that all the way from Copper's back. But, to his credit, he holds it together enough to guide Major into the ring. Greg follows on Merrylegs, I go third, and Joey follows behind on Blondie.

"Walk around a few times," Doug calls from the center of the ring. "Back straight, toes in, reins short, hands on top of the saddle."

Riding directly behind Greg, I copy his form down to the inch. But while I'm enjoying the opportunity to learn from the best, Barry has his hands full. Major refuses to cooperate, walking sideways and pulling strongly to the center of the ring, determined to take the day off.

"Shorten up on the reins," Doug calls.

"I am!" Barry calls back.

"Shorten some more!" Scott says.

With a bit of skill and maybe some luck, Barry finally gets Major to walk a full time around the ring. But just when Barry is probably getting comfortable, Scott ups the stakes.

"Let's see a trot," he calls.

Barry loosens the reins a half an inch and the horse is off, trotting fast.

"Pull back!" Doug calls.

Barry already is, in fact yanking on the reins so hard that Major is somehow trotting forward while looking sideways!

Despite being unable to see where he's going, the mighty horse keeps to the ring, moving faster and faster, until Barry has no choice but to let him canter. Then all bets are off. Rounding the curve, Major straightens his neck and stretches his legs to a full out gallop. Following behind, I lean forward in my saddle, feeling the wind rush, ducking under the low-lying branches that hang over the north end of the ring. We're breaking the rules, but who cares? It feels too good to matter. In seconds, Major has pulled up into the center of the ring and is clawing the grass. Then the rest of us are there, too, horses heaving, trotting sideways. All in all, a total meltdown.

Barry swings off of Major, hitting the ground hard.

"I'm not riding that horse anymore!"

Doug and Scott exchange a shrug.

"Okay," Scott says. "Switch with Greg."

It's the logical move: the best rider on the most difficult horse. But then Doug, my counselor and number one supporter, cuts in: "Nah, give Jackson a chance."

I'm so shocked I feel light-headed. "What? On *Major*?"

"Yep," Doug says.

Joey laughs. "He'll kill him! Rip his arms out of their sockets."

For the first time all summer, I agree with Joey Ambrose.

"What he said," I say. "I like having arms."

"Give it a try," Scott says.

Looks like I've interpreted his feelings about my sudden promotion to Group Three correctly. Scott doesn't think I'm ready. And now? I would either prove I belong or get my brains smashed in trying.

"Come on," Doug says. "Up you go."

I swing off Copper and walk with shaking legs over to Major.

"Good luck, bud," Barry says, handing me the reins.

"This gonna be nasty ugly," Joey proclaims with a grin.

It's hard to disagree. Barry and Greg remain stone still, like guests to an execution, while I shorten the stirrups. Then I

One Last Ride

swing onto the great horse. For a split second, I feel a rush of adrenaline. But that quick burst of excitement soon turns to mind-numbing fear. Major's a force of nature. And so tall! If I can't control him—or at least make a good stab at it—my entire summer will be exposed as a joke.

Doug helps me adjust my stirrups.

"Relax," he says. "You can do this." That's what I like about Doug: the quiet faith in his own decisions. While it doesn't calm me completely, it does give me enough confidence to nudge Major into the ring. Joey falls in behind me with Barry, now on Copper, and Greg, still on Merrylegs, taking up the rear.

"Just walk a few times around," Scott says. "Get used to it. If you stay calm, the horse will stay calm."

I want to believe him. But Major isn't the kind of animal to take emotional cues from his rider. Still, I try to control my breathing, try to enjoy being that high in that saddle, try to relax.

Then Major rears, just that suddenly and for no reason—there's no bird flying from the bushes, no chipmunk scurrying across the path. One minute he's walking, the next he's on his back legs, whinnying loudly.

"Hey!" I cry, barely holding on.

Wrestling with the reins I somehow get him pointed back toward the ring. After that, we walk twice around with no incident.

"Okay, how about a slow trot?" Doug calls.

Moving my hands forward, I give Major a light nudge with my heels, praying that I can keep him under wraps. And to my surprise, I do—for approximately three seconds. After that, I'm powerless to stop Major from pushing to a canter.

"Slow it down!" Scott calls.

I pull back on the reins as hard as I can. But unlike Barry, I'm not even strong enough to get Major to look sideways! Playtime is over. By the time we're rounding the corner Major is galloping, running full out, kicking up dirt, with nothing I can do about it. Worse, I can hear the other horses thundering behind me—an out and out break down. Then as the curve straightens, it happens: Major stumbles, only for a second, but long enough for a jolt of panic to explode through me. Is the horse going down? Like Caramel all those years ago? Thank God, Major rights himself quickly, swerves to the center of the ring, bucks once, then stops on a dime, sending me flying straight over his head like I've been shot out of catapult. In the air, I'm sure of a few things: I won't have to be in the horseshow, kiss Luna, or be emotionally destroyed if my parents break up—not with my brains leaking out of my ears. But the force of the mighty jolt twists me sideways and I land on my left side. As Scott and Doug rush over, the other kids pull their horses into the ring and jump off to help.

I look up, clutching my side, vision blurry. For a few seconds all I know is that the three boys and two counselors are leaning over me.

"He doesn't look dead at least," I finally hear Joey say. "That's better than I expected."

I've been thrown—badly. I'm going to have a nasty bruise, maybe even a limp for a while. But Joey is right: I'm not dead. And as my mind begins to clear, I see a new look in everyone's eyes. Concern and sympathy, of course, but also glimmers of something else: acceptance. In falling have I achieved what I wanted most? It looks that way.

"All right," Doug says. "Let's get you to the main house."

He picks me up and carries me all the way to Michelle's office: another benefit of that bad spill. For the second time in a single day, I'm going to have alone time with the best-looking woman in camp.

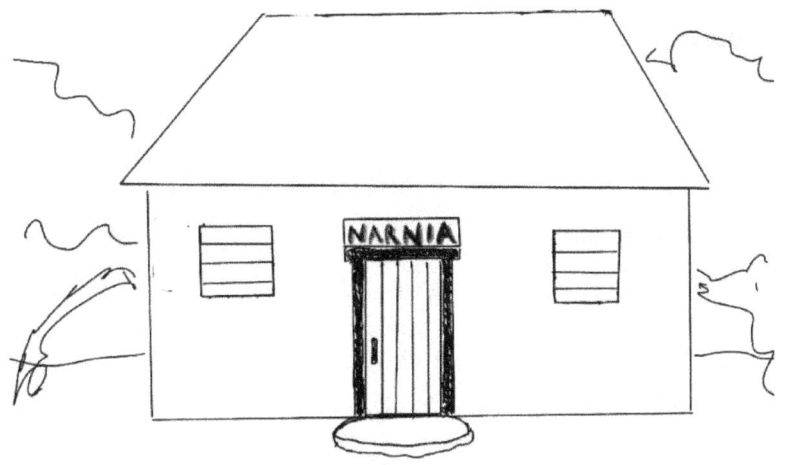

Chapter 11

At the evening bell I tuck in my shirt, lace my sneakers, and take a glance in the mirror to make sure my hair isn't sticking out in twenty different directions. Due to my dramatic dismount, I have this massive bruise on my hip and a slight limp that I've mostly walked off by lunch. But even though my body is basically okay, my psyche is another story. One minute I'm more excited than I've ever been, the next I'm more terrified. Even Mateo is surprised with the speed of the Pond Express: a return letter from Patti and Luna had arrived during eleven o'clock free swim. The upshot is that Ruth Bader Ginsberg is having their own game of Camp-Wide Capture the Flag that night, allowing the girls the freedom to sneak away as well. Just like that, it's game on. I'm sneaking out—to meet the assistant director's daughter!

A meeting is set for seven-thirty at Narnia, the girl's costume cabin.

"Hey, Mateo, why's it called Narnia anyway?"

That's one of a list of annoying questions I ask during rest hour. My friend glances up from his bunk where he may or may not have been using his pillow to prepare for the evening ahead. Then he answers as though he's addressing an idiot. Which he sort of is.

"Probably because someone liked the name from the book and decided to call it that."

You might say I'm nervous. To Mateo's credit, he answers other equally inane questions with surprising patience, a poster-boy for the cool and collected. But after dinner that goes away. See Mateo sometimes uses this hair gel which sits on his shelf in a yellow bottle. That night when he goes to dab some on he notices something: it's sticky. Further investigation reveals that someone has added in maple syrup. Of course, we all know who it is: Oliver. But does he admit it? No way.

"Relax, idiots," he says, when questioned. "I didn't touch your stupid gel."

Since Mateo discovers the syrup before he uses it, his hair lives to be wavy and purple another day. Still, he combs it six times (instead of the usual two or three) and tries on four t-shirts before finally settling on a light blue polo—sure signs that even he is feeling the pressure. Still terrified, I can't keep my mouth shut.

"What's Luna going to be wearing?"

We're standing by woodcraft by then, on the way to RBG. The minute the words are out of my mouth, I realize that I've pushed too far. Mateo looks so annoyed, I half worry he's going to grab an axe and throw me down on the chopping block. And I enjoy having a head.

"Sorry," I say, quickly. "Stupid question."

"You think?" Mateo says. "I mean, I imagine that she'll be wearing clothes."

"I said it was stupid already."

Mateo sighs. "Listen, I know this is new for you, okay? But do me a favor."

"Sure, a favor. What?"

"Try and have fun tonight. Can you do that for me, Jackson? Have some fun?"

"Sure," I stammer. "Fun."

I glance toward the main house where the rest of the camp is gathering to choose sides for Capture the Flag. That's the sort of "fun" a kid my age is supposed to be having, right? Part of me is desperate to join in. The trouble is that alongside that boy who still wants to run and play, there's this highly hormonal dude who's after just the sort of "fun" Mateo has in mind.

So as the counselors divide sides into shirts and skins, Mateo and I sneak behind the post-office and cross the camp lane. I almost turn back. What if Lou is out prowling? What if Luna and I are caught by her own father?

"Hey, Mateo," I say, as he turns up the dirt road to the farm.

"What?" Mateo says, wheeling around. "You don't wanna go back, do you?"

"Of course I don't. I'm all in, man!"

What else can I say? Fear of looking like a coward in front of my friend outweighs my fear of getting caught. Thankfully, once we're on the dirt road, out of sight of the rest of camp, I manage to relax—or let's just say I try as hard as I can. Soon we're climbing the pasture gate. It's hard to believe that the dance had only been a short night earlier.

"No talking to that horse tonight," Mateo warns me as I looked across Cowpatty Field at Merrylegs, flanked by Major and Copper. "We're going straight to the girls."

Mateo is right. Tonight's about the ladies. My first date ever. So I follow my friend down the pasture past archery. Once we hit the pine forest, he cuts off of the path into the woods.

"What're you doing?" I ask.

"Can't enter through the gate," Mateo says. "Could be counselors around."

We bushwhack through rows of pine trees and bushes, veering deeper into the lower pasture, further and further from the path to the RBG gate. Just when I'm about to ask when far is far enough, he crouches behind a bush.

"There it is," he says, pointing.

"What?"

"The RBG border."

I look ahead, only to see rows and rows of trees.

"Where's the fence?"

"There isn't one down here. We just go in."

I swallow hard. It couldn't be that easy.

"And then what?"

"We go to Narnia."

"And you know where that is, right?"

Strangely, I haven't thought to ask that earlier.

Mateo brushes his hair out of his eyes. "It's by the wash house."

That sounds like dangerous territory, raising images of girls wrapped in post-shower towels or, God Forbid, using toilets!

"And you know where this wash house is?"

"Not really," Mateo says.

Not the answer I'm expecting.

"Not *really*?" I gasp.

"We'll find it."

"How?"

Mateo grins. "It's a washhouse, idiot. We'll smell it."

Panic is returning. From day one of the summer Mateo has come off as a kid who knows things.

"Anyway," Mateo says. "Better get ready."

"Ready?" I ask.

I have on a clean pair of jeans, t-shirt, and actual sneakers. How much more ready can a twelve-year-old be?

"Yeah," Mateo says. "Ready. As in, French Foreign legion."

One Last Ride

With that, he stands by a tree, unzips his fly and pees—a common enough thing at a boy's camp but not one I expect a moment before an illegal meeting with two girls.

"French Foreign Legion?"

Mateo shrugs. "I heard some Cabin nine kids call it that. Do you have to go?"

I do. So I find my own tree, unzip and get to business.

"Make extra sure not to drip on your pants," Mateo says.

"Duh," I say.

The truth is that I already have, wetting my underwear. Thank God for small miracles. Wearing black jeans, the spot won't be noticeable.

"You done?" Mateo asks.

I zip. I tuck. I nod.

"Done."

I will myself to stay upbeat, confident. Yes, Mateo's unsure of Narnia's exact location but how hard can it be to find? There's no backing out now. I've even marked my territory.

"Follow me," Mateo says.

Even though it's called Camp-Wide Capture the Flag, the unwritten rule is that the players stick to the parts of camp in everyday use—not the acres and acres owned by the Jones' family, left to grow wild. Even so, Mateo and I walk as silently as we can, ducking under occasional low-drooping branches until the RBG border is only twenty feet away. Then just as I'm relaxing into the moment, even maybe enjoying it, Mateo pulls up short, grabs my shirt and says, "Shhh!"

I stop, heart pounding.

"What?"

"Quiet."

We're dead still, the only sound is the wind rustling through the leaves. Then we hear it: a distant giggle. Not the giggle of a young girl, but someone older.

Mateo drops behind a large rock like he's taken a cannonball to his gut, pulling me beside him. Just in time, too. To my surprise, Scott Hill, the head of riding, appears through the trees no more than thirty feet away. More surprising still, he's holding hands with a woman I recognize as being the head of the girl's ranch. It all comes to me: overheard conversations at the riding ring about Doug's girlfriend, Courtney, and someone else named Jeanne. I've thought that she was someone from back home, maybe a girlfriend from college—but apparently an inter-ranch romance is in play and Scott and Jeanne are also cutting out on Camp Wide Capture the Flag to meet. I have to admit that it gives me a certain feeling of power to watch two counselors I know, actual twenty-somethings, walk through the woods, assuming that they are alone and unobserved. Then more exciting, not to mention embarrassing, they stop and kiss, thankfully not for long, then laugh again and keep on walking, arms around each other's waists. By the time they disappear out of sight, Mateo and I are grinning like mad.

"Scott has a girlfriend," Mateo says.

"Sure does," I answer.

"See what I mean?" Mateo punches my shoulder. "Everything loosens up around here the last week. Now come on."

Seeing Scott and Jeanne does wonders for my confidence. If two counselors can sneak off, why not two campers? And what really would happen if we were caught anyway? Would they send us home? Camp ends in just five days, right?

Mateo and I hurry into RBG territory, then cut back up through their woods toward the main grounds. I don't know if Mateo really knows where he's going or just gets lucky, but we soon come upon a small building. A few steps closer, I see the sign: the Killington Washhouse.

"Told you," Mateo whispers.

A minute later he leads us smack into another cabin, this one situated about forty feet from the RBG gate. Set slightly off in the woods, I've passed it unnoticed on the way to every dance all summer. Heading around the front, we see the sign hanging on the door: NARNIA. I'm stunned. I had assumed that we wouldn't find it; that like spies behind enemy lines, we'd get lost then have to bushwhack back to Flying Eagle, mission unaccomplished. Instead, here we are. My belief in Mateo Greene returns.

"Yo, dude! Nice!"

We slap five. Then slap again.

"You ready?" Mateo asks.

Without waiting for my answer (I'm not ready), he pushes open the door, revealing a small room with an overhead loft filled with discarded clothing and costumes. Underneath the loft are boxes filled with more clothes. That's it, no hangers, no shelves, just boxes, like a messy lost and found in a church basement. In its own way, RBG is just as low rent as Flying Eagle.

"Hello?" Mateo whispers.

I'm stone still. Nothing.

"They aren't here," he says.

I exhale heavily, relieved. Perhaps this is the best result—I get credit for being brave, being one of the guys, but I don't have to face Luna in the flesh in a dark cabin.

"What time is it?" I ask.

Another stupid question—neither of us wears a watch.

"Don't know," Mateo says. "Around the right time."

"You think they're coming?"

"They're coming."

"You're sure?"

"Yes."

"What do we do while we wait?"

The way Mateo sees it there are two options: stand there in the half-dark or look through the clothes. Just to say it, Mateo and I don't set out to actually get *in* costume. But what begins as harmless joking around, holding up coats and men's breeches to each other's bodies, soon turns into daring each other to try something on. Before we know it we're pulling on actual clothes, desperately trying to muffle laughter. Mateo's dressed in a Revolutionary era coat, wearing a white wig that makes him look like a modern-day founding father. And me? Carrying a musket, I'm dressed in a pair of riding boots that hikes all the way up to my thighs and an army helmet. Which is when both Mateo and I sort of read each other's minds. I guess good friends can do that. Right on cue, we begin to sing one of the main raps from the musical *Hamilton*. Why not? We're dressed for the era, right?

I am not throwing away my shot!
I am not throwing away my shot!

Then before I know it, I have a brainstorm.
"Mateo. This is it: our shower announcement!"
"What?" he says. "*I am not throwing away my shot?*"
"No, we change the lyrics!"
I let it fly:
I am not throwing away my soap!
I am not throwing away my soap!

Clever or not, at that moment, giddy with the excitement of making it all the way to Narnia, it seems sort of brilliant. And Mateo gets onboard right away. We slap five then sing it together. More like shout it:
I am not throwing away my soap!
I am not throwing away my soap!

Then I go on:

I am just like my buddy
Filthy, mucky, muddy
I am not throwing away my...

Which is when the door swings open.

Chapter 12

"Keep it down, guys! I can hear you all the way to the path!"

I see the outline of a girl. It's Patti.

"Sorry," Mateo says.

We've stopped singing. But laughing? That we can't control.

"You guys," she says, covering her mouth. I think her eyes have adjusted enough to see how we're dressed.

I have to hand it to Mateo. He has the confidence to take any embarrassing situation and run with it.

"What?" he says, strutting across the floor. "I don't remind you of George Washington?"

Patti laughs. "Um...no?"

Which is when I notice. She's alone.

"Hey," I say. "Where's Luna?"

For a split second I worry that she's seen me in an army hat, carrying a gun and run for her life. Then I look to Patti. I don't remember seeing someone look that uncomfortable since the day my mom finally admitted that she and my dad were on the skids.

"What?" I ask.

Patti is staring to the side, unable to meet my eyes. "Listen, Jackson. She sort of bagged out."

"Bagged out?"

For some reason it's hard to comprehend. Sure, she had stood up Oliver—*but that was Oliver*!

"Yeah," Patti says.

"You mean, she's not coming?"

I still can't quite get it through my thick head.

"But she really likes you," Patti says.

"But she's not coming?" I repeat.

Patti shakes her head. "Sorry."

I'm stunned. What of our epic slow-dance? The tetherball games? Our wedding with Lin Manuel Miranda?

"She still likes you," Mateo says. "That's cool, right?"

"Right," Patti repeats. "She told me."

"Then why isn't she here?" I ask. "She chickened out?"

"Her dad is your assistant director," Patti says.

"I know," I shout. "Which is why I almost didn't come, but I did!"

"Sorry," Patti says. "She got nervous."

Mateo slaps my back. "You hear that? This is good!"

"*Good?*"

"Think about it: Luna gets nervous and you get nervous. More proof that you two are perfect for each other."

If there is a dim point in there somewhere I'm in no mood to hear it.

"What good does it do me if we're both nervous but in two different places?"

One Last Ride

Feeling equal parts anger and self-pity, I reach for the door. But with my hand on the knob, I hear something—footsteps!

The three of us freeze and meet eyes. Then I grin wildly. Because I know just who it is...

Luna!

She's realized her mistake! In seconds she'll burst through the door and kiss me so hard the cabin will catch on fire.

"It's her," I whisper.

Mateo and Patti know better. In a flash they're up the ladder to the loft and buried underneath a pile of costumes. As for me, I'm so confident that I yank open the door myself.

"Hey there!"

It isn't Luna.

"Lou?" I stammer.

I should have known that he would be on the prowl. As assistant director, programming and discipline are his main duties. I swallow hard, caught red handed. Luckily, Lou seems more amused than mad, not to mention a little bit surprised. It's like he had expected to find someone else, probably someone older—and sure not someone in costume. At least I'm not wearing one of the tutus.

"Jackson?" he says, scratching his mustache. "What brings you to the girl's costume shop?"

He's smiling by then but still refrains from asking why I'm dressed for Lexington and Concord. What can I do? Say that I had gotten lost and been forced to play dress up? There's no way out but the truth—or at least half of it.

"I'm here to meet someone. She didn't show up."

Lou nods. Does he know that the "someone" is his own daughter? Probably. But I soon realize that he isn't there to embarrass me anymore than I already am. Besides, even if he knows, I doubt he has any specific objections to me and Luna—his objections have to do with skipping Capture the Flag.

He glances toward the loft. "Anyone else here with you?"

"No," I say, immediately. "I came alone."

I doubt he believes me, but he probably doesn't care

enough to climb up the ladder and poke around under a bunch of costumes. Things really do loosen up during the last week.

"Okay, then," he says. "Get back to Flying Eagle. Pick a side and join the game."

"Yeah," I say. "Capture the Flag. Sure."

I move quickly for the door, thrilled to get off with nothing more than an order to do something I like. Then Lou clears his throat.

I stop, heart pounding.

"Yeah?"

He places a hand on my shoulder. "Leave the fake musket here, son. It might give some people he wrong idea."

With that, he's nice enough to leave so I can change in peace. As I toss my costume up to the loft, Mateo whispers down, "Thanks for covering!"

Feeling a weird mixture of regret, embarrassment, and relief, I push out the door and run all the way back to the Flying Eagle pasture. Yeah, Lou has let me off scot free. But once I join the game, as a shirt, it isn't long before I receive my punishment: tagged behind enemy lines, I spend most of the evening in jail. I never have a chance to make a single attempt on the skin's flag.

Chapter 13

Ever seen videos of those crazy guys who seal themselves in a barrel and shoot over Niagara Falls? They tend to start where the water's calm, right? Just before it gets rough. Then as the rapids become more powerful, they pick up speed, going faster and faster until they're thundering down the river like a rocket and then...boom! Out they go over the spray.

That's how the summer was feeling. Weeks one through seven I was just sort of floating along, minding my own business. But when I met Luna at the start of week eight? That's when I hit the first rapids. Nabbed in Narnia? The rapids began to churn faster. Still, it isn't until the day after Capture the Flag that I hit the point of no return. Yes, I've been caught with an army hat and fake musket, but what happens the next morning is more public. More humiliating, too.

To start off, I'm in a foul mood. Can you blame me? I had taken a big risk, after all, gone undercover and sneaked to the RBG costume cabin. Luna, on the other hand, had decided I wasn't worth that risk. Oliver devotes breakfast to rubbing it in. Sure, Mateo tries to cheer me up (while making sure to tell me that he and Patti had broken their make-out record by four and a half minutes), but the bottom line is this: Luna cared more about getting caught and punished than seeing the new love of her life. Which gets me thinking: maybe I'm *not* the love of her life. Maybe she doesn't like me as much as I like her? By the time announcements are over, I feel pretty darned low. After breakfast, while changing for riding back in the cabin, that sadness boils down to rage. I walk to the ranch practically raving, discovering the twisted pleasure of nursing a heartbreak by lashing out at the heartbreaker. Luna? Who the heck is she? A mal-formed girl with a gum line so noticeable it can be seen from the third moon of Jupiter, that's who! A crazy psychopath who wears politically correct T-shirts she probably doesn't even believe in to lure young liberals into her arms! A self-absorbed lowlife who has used me for my body! For a single slow-dance! As Joey Ambrose would say: tyranny!

By the time I reach the ranch I'm mad at the world. Uncontrolled rage can lead otherwise sane people—in theory me—to take wild, unnecessary risks.

Bareback.

Doug had first offered me the chance a week earlier but I didn't think I was ready—too easy to fall off, too easy to wrack myself—my crotch, if you know what I mean, a place no guy likes being wracked. But my current mind-set has nothing to do with self-preservation and everything to do with acting out, taking a risk, any risk really, to prove to Luna how little I care about her.

"Doug?" I say, after helping saddle horses for Group One. "I'm ready. Bareback today?"

Boy, does he look surprised.

"You sure about that?"

"Yeah," I say. "Positive."

What could go wrong? I'm a good rider, right? I've advanced quickly. And hasn't Doug already explained to me basic rules of bareback safety? As he helps me onto Merrylegs, he shows me again.

"Grab the reins as usual, okay? Squeeze hard with your upper legs so you don't bounce around. You don't want to accidentally sit on anything."

I smile grimly.

"That wouldn't be fun."

"It isn't," Doug says. "Okay, then. Start by walking around the field outside the ring."

It feels strange to be atop a horse with no saddle but not as uncomfortable as I had expected. And Merrylegs, on her best behavior, takes it slow, walking nice and easy.

"How's it feel?" Doug calls over.

"Good," I call back.

Now don't get me wrong, I'm still angry at Luna. Furious. But that doesn't stop me from imagining that she's there that very second, standing by the hitching posts, awestruck by my stunning technique as I guide Merrylegs around the field, my brown hair waving handsomely in the morning wind.

"Is this really the first time you've gone bareback?" I imagine her calling to me.

"You got that right," I answer. "No sweat."

I swing around and ride backwards.

Then I stand on my head and Luna shrieks and claps her hands.

"Do a back flip!" she calls.

Who am I to refuse?

After executing a dismount worthy of an Olympic gold medalist, I imagine running into her waiting arms. Life is funny sometimes. It's almost as though thinking about Luna conjures her up for real. Because just then I hear a neigh—not from our riding ring or Merrylegs either, but from another horse coming up the path from below the ranch. Every other day or so, during morning activities, the RBG girls take trail rides, passing through Flying Eagle on their way to the back woods. Still on Merrylegs, I look over my shoulder. At the front, atop a large white horse, is Jeanne, Scott's girlfriend. Behind her is a row of girls. Suddenly, Luna is there, too, atop a small grey pony with a white spot on his forehead. Worse, she's wearing another of her politically correct T-shirts: "I LOVE PEOPLE WHO HATE FRACKING!"

How can I stay mad at a girl like that? Doesn't she know what those sorts of sentiments do to an environmentally conscious New York City boy?

"Hey," she calls.

"Hey!" I call back.

"What's up?" Jeanne calls over to Doug. "Letting the kids go bareback today?"

"Nah," Doug calls back. "Jackson just wanted to try it. He's our most improved rider this year."

It's a nice thing of him to say and I was flattered, for sure—especially since Luna hears it all.

"Hey, Jackson," she says. "Sorry about last night."

"That's all right," I lie. "No biggie."

I'm struck once again by Luna's looks. She's cute and quirky and big nosed and smiley in a way that pushes whatever twelve-year-old buttons I have to be pushed. How can I stay angry at a girl like that?

"Nice horse," she calls.

"Yeah. Merrylegs is the greatest."

No sooner are the words out of my mouth than that great horse decides that it's her moment to get more involved in that morning's drama. I'll never know why she spooks at that precise moment. Had she seen a chipmunk? A bird? Who knows? Whatever the reason, Merrylegs suddenly sidesteps and begins a mad trot for the Flying Eagle stables. For a heartbeat, I'm happy. Now Luna can see how well I ride. But easier said than done. Merrylegs goes from a walk to a trot so suddenly that it's a struggle to simply stay on. Then I lose my balance and lurch forward.

Which is when I experience firsthand why most guys don't like riding bareback. Doug is right: sitting on yourself is most definitely not fun. Especially when it's with the full force of your body weight. Especially when that weight comes down on your nuts three times in rapid succession.

Whack!

Whack!

Whack!

I cry out and roll off of Merrylegs' back. Hitting the ground like a sack of rocks, I ball up in a fetal position and moan. The next thing I know, Doug is at my side, helping me, but laughing.

"Hey, Jackson? You okay?"

Out of the corner of my eye I see Luna wrinkle her brow, concerned, amused, or confused, I can't tell.

"Are you all right?" she calls over.

"He's fine," Doug replies, covering for me. "Just hurt his knee."

I doubt she believes him. Still, she smiles my way and calls, "Feel better!" Then the girls are gone and Doug is leaning close.

"You whacked yourself good, huh?"

I let loose another animal moan. Doug smiles.

"A boyhood rite of passage," he says. "Check it off your list."

With that, he all but carries me to the bench by the hitching post. Then he glances back to where the girls have just ridden through.

"Luna Hart was on that trail ride?"

I nod. I mean, it's still hard to form words.

"Don't worry," he says. "I doubt she had any idea what was going on. She probably knows less about guys than you know about girls."

"You think?" I manage, hopefully.

Doug tousles my hair. "When you feel better let me know

and you can ride again." Then I guess he can't resist. "Maybe with a saddle this time."

It takes a while to feel better. Under normal circumstances, calculating for speed, weight, and directness of impact, one solid whack probably would've been enough to keep a kid like me down for the count for a good ten minutes. But three in a row? Direct hits? I'm on the bench for the rest of first period and most of the second, breathing deeply through my nose, trying not to puke. Then just when I'm feeling well enough to imagine standing up, the morning's drama turns from a painful comedy to a heart-crunching tragedy.

Most days the mail arrives early at Flying Eagle, often by ten AM. That gives the head of the camp post office and handyman, an old-timer named Pete time to sort it out before eleven o' clock swim. If the mail comes earlier, Pete likes to walk it around to the activities where he knows certain kids are likely to be.

So it isn't all that strange to see him round the corner to the ranch in his jeans and dirty work boots with a hand delivery or two for either Doug, Scott, Greg, Joey, Barry, me, or some of the other people who live and die by the horses. That particular day I'm so focused on the pain in my crotch that I don't see him until the last second.

"Hey, Jackson, boy," he says. "What happened to you?"

Another thing about Pete. He adds the word "boy" to everyone's name.

Considering that I'm still doubled over on the bench, "What happened to you?" is a fair question.

"Rode a horse bareback," I croak. To my credit, I manage eye contact and a smile. "Cracked myself pretty hard."

Pete is a native Vermonter through and through. Loosely translated, he has a certain talent for understatement.

"Yep," he says with a simple nod. "That probably hurt a bit. Maybe this'll cheer you up."

He tosses an envelope on my lap. My mom. Most days I'm perfectly happy to get a letter from home. My mother's letters are friendly enough, short and dashed off, but filled with whatever breezy news she can think to include then signed, "Be Good" or "Have Fun" with a handful of x's and o's. As far as I remember, that day's letter is the same as them all—friendly and mostly forgettable. I read it quickly then get back to focusing on my slow but steady recovery. But then I see something. The upper left-hand corner of the envelope, the return address. Usually, my mom scrawls a quick, "Segal, 325 East 77th St.," our home since I was born. Looking more closely, I blink, temporarily stunned. The name is the same but the address?

14 W. 89th St. Apt. 14C.

West 89th Street? That's uptown and across the park, no man's land, a neighborhood I've probably been in all of four times in my entire life! What the heck is my mother doing putting down that return address? Has she made a mistake? Had a seizure and forgotten where we lived?

The news is so big that it takes a long moment to sink into my disbelieving cranium. I stare at the address, dazed, stupefied and otherwise bewildered because there's only one explanation that makes any sense:

She's moved!

Which is when the tragic finale to that morning's drama officially kicks into gear. Sure, I know my parents are having troubles. They've told me that. I mean, they were barely talking by the time they left on visiting day. But the idea of them doing something drastic like actually separating is too big a concept for me to wrap my head around.

But now? There's no denying reality. If the time I had cried to Michelle after visiting day was a summer rainstorm, this is a hurricane. In a way it's lucky: doubled over, I'm already in the customary wailing position. But now the pain in my groin comes in second to the one in my heart. As tears gush out of me, my body shakes. Once again—and this seemed to be happening a lot lately—Doug is at my side, arm around my shoulder. In the beginning he thinks I had re-ruptured myself, maybe gotten kicked by one of the horses. But soon enough, through a series of incoherent grunts and maybe a few words, I let him know what is happening. Thankfully, Doug knows what to do. Sometimes a person just needs space to be sad. Sometimes there are no words. For a few minutes, Doug doesn't say a thing, just comforts me by being there. When the bell for eleven o'clock swim rings and I'm still crying, Doug waves Scott and a few other curious kids away to unsaddle the horses and lead them back to the stalls. Only when everyone has cleared out and my tears have become sniffles, does Doug weigh in.

"I know that address looks bad, but you can't truly know what it means, not yet, anyway."

"I know," I say. "But it may not be good, right?"

Doug nods. "It may not be good."

I have to give him points for honesty.

"But maybe it's not as bad as I think?" I say hopefully. "Maybe my mom moved her office or something?"

I know it isn't true. Her office is in midtown and has been for years.

"Maybe," Doug says. "It's always best not to jump to conclusions."

We sit silently for another minute.

"You know," Doug says, looking straight ahead to the riding ring. "My parents divorced when I was a kid."

It is a surprise. I know about Courtney—Doug talks about her a fair amount—but not much else. It's almost as though he sprung to life fully formed to be my counselor.

"How old were you?"

"Younger than you. Nine or so. And it was hard."

That isn't what I wanted to hear.

"Oh, great," I say.

Doug smiles. "Let me finish. I'm trying to say that you don't know what's going to happen. But if it does go wrong, it'll be hard but you'll get through it. You'll be okay."

I had thought that Doug had taken me under his wing

because I was in his cabin and had fallen in love with riding. But maybe he knows what's going on at home, too. My parents had to have mentioned it to Harvey when they dropped me off. Maybe Doug has been keeping an eye out for me from the beginning?

"Thanks," I say.

"Anytime. You ready?"

Before I can respond, I feel something wet and soft on my face, like I'm getting scrubbed by a soft bristled brush.

Merrylegs!

I stand for the first time in an hour and wrap my arms around her neck.

"I'd say someone cares about you," Doug says.

It's hard to believe. She couldn't have backed out of her stall to see if I was okay, could she? But what other explanation is there?

"I guess so."

The last thing I want is for Doug to see me tear up again, this time over a stupid horse, so I lead Merrylegs by her halter back to her stall. Then Doug gives me a few moments alone with her before he calls my name. I give Merrylegs a final hug before walking out, then Doug and I walk side by side down the dirt road, past the farm to the main yard. By the time we get there it's almost time for lunch. A small consolation: Tuesday's are my favorite, Sloppy Joes.

Chapter 14

That afternoon at rest hour, Harvey Jones puts on a show. After sniffing his way through the front door, he checks in on Garth's book collection, focusing on a well-worn copy of a Michael Jordan biography. Then, once he's finished the sports history lesson, he jumps onto Noah's trunk and begins to scurry back and forth, staying longer than usual, until Rusty gets the idea to crank his radio.

"Let's give that guy a beat to work with," he says.

To our collective amazement, Harvey Jones starts to time his scurries to the music—that's how it seems—once even rising to his hind legs and waving his paws over his head! A dancing chipmunk? Why not? It isn't long before we're cheering, stamping, and clapping along. Then Noah begins a chant, "Har-vey! Har-vey! Har-vey!" For a brief moment, he goes even faster, feeding off our energy. But maybe the spotlight isn't for him or maybe we're just too loud: seconds later, he freezes, leaps off the trunk and shoots through a crack in the wall.

After that, Noah takes a turn dancing on his trunk while Oliver and Mateo have a towel fight. Only then do we finally get around to doing what we are supposed to be doing: resting. I'm reading when Doug sits on the edge of my bunk. It's hard to blame him for looking more serious than usual: that morning I had cried so hard I had blown snot all over his sleeve.

"Flying Eagle doesn't usually let campers call home," he begins. "You know that, right?"

"Yeah, I know."

Everyone knows it. It says so in the brochure in bold lettering.

"But there are some exceptions," Doug says. "For emergencies."

I see where he is headed.

"This isn't an emergency."

Doug looks surprised. "You got a letter with a new return address. You don't know who's picking you up or if your parents are still together."

A lump in my throat comes back. Maybe some of my cabinmates have already heard about my breakdown at the ranch, but the last thing I want is to bawl again right there in front of them. That's a humiliation a twelve-year-old boy would give a kidney to avoid.

"Yeah, so?" I stammer.

"So go ahead," Doug says. "Run up to Sunrise."

Michelle's cabin. "Why? You think she's heard from my parents today?"

"Probably not," Doug says. "But she's in charge of pick-ups, right? So she can ask Harvey for permission for you to call home."

Michelle had offered to do the same thing the previous

morning. Part of me still doesn't want to know anything more about what's happening in New York—not yet anyway. I just can't face it. Then again, the letter has changed things. Despite a better than average lunch of Sloppy Joes and the dancing of our cabin mascot, my future hasn't been far from my thoughts. How often will I see my dad? Will I *ever* see my dad? Will I live with my dad and never see my mom? Will my mom join a cult? Will my dad go vegan? Worst of all, will they get re-married? During afternoon announcements I had fantasized about a double wedding, my parents side by side, exchanging vows with their new partners: a pair of blind dwarves. You might say that I'm losing it. Or maybe I had just listened to Garth go on about *The Lord of the Rings* one time too many. The point is this: curiosity is out-weighing fear. If there's a way to find out what's truly going on at home, why not take it? Maybe there's an explanation I haven't thought of? Maybe my mom's office really has moved? Maybe she and my dad are investing in real estate? Maybe she had been high on cough medicine and written down a friend's address by accident? Anything is possible.

"Okay," I say. "You're right."

Doug smiles. "Good. Head on up to Sunrise and tell Michelle I say it's okay."

"Now?" I say.

"Yeah. Go find out. You'll feel better."

I get up, but not without worrying about what my bunkmates will think. Getting excused from rest hour is rare. And to those who haven't already heard about my dramatic breakdown, I'm not in the mood to confess the scene at the ranch. Luckily, Doug is a step ahead of me.

"Jackson's hip is hurting from when he fell off the horse yesterday. He's going to Michelle to check it out."

If I think I can just quietly sneak out after that, boy am I ever mistaken. An excuse to visit Michelle at any hour is a privilege. But during rest hour? That's hitting the jackpot. Never underestimate the power of a good-looking, friendly twenty-something woman on a boy.

"Michelle?" Noah calls out. "That's no fair!"

"A bad hip is nothing!" Oliver says. "My elbow is killing me! I have to see Michelle, too. Come on, Doug!"

"Elbow?" Garth says, holding out his glasses. "I need a new prescription. Plus, I have a scab on my knee!"

"I've been combing my hair too much," Mateo says. "I think I have lice. Maybe maggots."

"I've got rabies, okay?" Noah bellows, jumping to the floor with a giant crash. Gay or not, it doesn't matter, Michelle has cast a spell over him, too. "I might start frothing any minute, all right? I might not last the day!"

Doug reacts like I knew he would, with calm laughter. Then Rusty picks Noah up over his shoulder (no mean feat) and deposits him on his bunk. Meanwhile, I limp dramatically out the door. But once I'm out of sight I jog past Cabin One, more excited than I am probably willing to admit about yet another opportunity to visit our ridiculously pretty nurse. So I start running, cruising past the main house then up the steep hill toward the upper flats where the youngest campers live.

Sunrise stands down a windy path through the woods, next to an unused tennis court, cracked at the edges, with weeds growing out of the service lines. Still running all out, I recite my mom and dad's cell numbers—luckily, I still remember them both—ready to find out whatever news I can. I want the facts, plain and simple. No more wondering what my life is going to be in four days. Everything will soon be revealed.

Winded, I slow to a walk down the path to Sunrise, about twenty feet from the cabin. Catching my breath, I hear a light creak from inside, footsteps on a wood floor. I smile. Michelle is home. In seconds, she'll march me down to Harvey Jones and demand, "Give this young man a phone!" Then another creak is followed by a giggle. Definitely Michelle! Probably chuckling at something she's reading. No doubt about it: she's there. So I keep on going, moving quickly until an altogether different sound reaches my ears: not a creak or a giggle, but a gasp.

One Last Ride

I stop short, momentarily confused, but smart enough to know that I'm treading in dangerous territory. Unable to resist, I drop slowly to my knees where I can see though the slats of the cabin. By pure dumb luck (or unlucky luck) I find myself peering directly into the bedroom. Yes, it's a narrow view, but still enough to get an eyeful...of Michelle...making out with Jay Kreigel—the head of weavery.

I can't believe it. Michelle with a skinny non-descript dude who teaches boys how to work a loom? A guy whose job at camp is to make wall hangings and rugs? I mean, if Michelle had a boyfriend wouldn't he have been Tad Riggins, the head of athletics? Or Don Handley, the freakishly muscular assistant cook? But no—Michelle likes her guys skinny, unathletic, and creative—inotherwords, guys like *me*.

I know what might be about to happen. My father had told me the facts of life when I was in fourth grade, a conversation that had left me ready to hurl.

"Go," I tell myself. "Get out of here!"

But I can't—not without looking a little bit longer. So I take a step forward...right onto a stick.

Crack!

Fast as a cat, Jay looks to the wall of the cabin—thank God there isn't a window—and freezes. I freeze, too, then run like I'm being chased by an alien army, tearing back up the path, then diving behind a giant oak tree just as the front door swings open.

"Hello?" he calls.

Part of me wants to throw myself at his mercy and confess everything. That would've been the right thing to do, wouldn't it? But I can't do that. What will Jay say if he finds out I was snooping? Worse, what would he *do*? Stick my head in a loom and knit me into a tapestry?

"Anyone there?" I hear Michelle call.

Jay looks again. "No, don't think so."

"Then come on back. It's probably just a chipmunk."

I exhale deeply, not realizing that I've been holding my

breath. Thank God: Sunrise has their own Harvey Jones to contend with. The door closes and I sit where I am, shaking, heart pounding. I have to tell my cabin what I've seen, right? Michelle and Jay kissing! That's too good to keep to myself! But on the other hand, how can I rat out someone like Michelle who has been so nice to me? I need time to think. When I'm sure the coast is clear, I creep back out to the upper flats, then hightail it past cabins Gale and Breeze, the little kids, and down to the pasture where I flop down in the middle of the ballfield, flat on my back, and gaze up at the sky, wondering what to do next.

That's when I realize that maybe Michelle's sex life has done me a favor. Maybe it's given me the extra time I need to truly figure out how I want to handle the situation with my parents. I mean, why call home at all? Because what if my suspicions are right? What if my mother has moved out? I'll be devastated, right? The end of camp will be ruined. As it stands now, I have four full days left to enjoy life pre-divorce: the horseshow, the final hike day, the fair. And yes, Luna had stood me up just like she stood up Oliver, but hadn't she called out, "Sorry about last night" as she had ridden by? That's an apology, isn't it? And hadn't she seemed happy to see me? Doesn't that mean that we might re-connect at the fair? Talk, hug, hold hands—who knows? If my parents are splitting, I have the rest of my life to be miserable. Why not enjoy four more days at camp pain free?

So I lay there in the pasture until the end of rest hour, blotting out anything having to do with home, slowly gathering myself to re-enter camp life. When the bell for afternoon activities rings, I know what I need to fully clear my head: a soothing swim and paddle in a kayak. Besides, an older kid has told me that there's a dead body in the neck of the pond. I doubt it's true—no way Harvey Jones would let a body decay in the water where the kids' swim—but it still seems worth exploring.

So off I go, out of the pasture and down the dirt road. In

the main yard, I run into Doug, headed my way to lead the afternoon trail ride.

"Any luck with Michelle?" he calls.

We stop in front of the post office.

I shake my head. "Nobody was home."

"Really?"

I hate to lie, but what other choice do I have?

"Maybe mom was taking a nap. Anyway, I think I'm all right. I'll just wait and see."

Doug looks surprised. "You sure that's what you want? I can just ask Harvey myself for permission to call home."

"Yeah...I mean, thanks, but...I think I just want to enjoy the rest of camp, you know?"

Doug thinks about it for a second then nods. "I can understand that. But if you need to talk, let me know."

I'm still desperate to tell someone what I had seen up at Sunrise, but I know how mean that would be. All I can do now is hope that Doug never mentions to Michelle that he sent me to her cabin and that Jay hadn't seen me dive behind that tree.

"Sure," I say. "Thanks."

I watch Doug walk down the road until he's out of sight. Then I change and head to the pond. I don't find that dead body. Then again I never expect to.

Chapter 15

That night is the annual election for the camp mascot, a wild event that shakes the lodge almost to the ground. The candidates are Norman, a sweet sheep, and Trudi, the camp cow. I guess people don't want a mascot with an udder disease. Norman takes the "cute" vote to an easy win.

Then the next morning, Wednesday, is the horse show. Just like I predicted, I come in last. Worse, due to a random drawing of straws, I'm stuck with Major. Neither of us is pleased. He doesn't buck me off, but Doug has to hold his reins between the walk, trot, and canter events to keep him still—the ultimate humiliation. As for the other members of Group Three, they place in the order I predicted and react exactly as I expect: Joey cares less that his ribbon is yellow, Barry is pleased enough with second place and Greg smiles happily, trying to act surprised with a first place finish everyone with half a brain knew was coming.

Things get a little bit better at lunch when our Cabin performs my Hamilton inspired shower-rap. It doesn't really follow much from the show but it has some okay lines.

Get so clean
It'll be obscene
Get a dirt vaccine
For a shiny sheen.

Stuff like that.

At the end, we all jump on our table and lead the camp in a crazed cheer.

I AM NOT THROWING AWAY MY SOAP!
I AM NOT THROWING AWAY MY SOAP!

After my last place finish in the horse show, it's nice to get a little love.

Anyway, Flying Eagle doesn't have an annual Color War but that doesn't mean that there aren't tons of other activities designed to rile a group of boys into a frenzy. There are swim meets, boat races, skit nights, Capture the Flag, and Capture the Counselor. And then there's the psycho-scream fest called the Holiday Farms game.

I had made the team because everyone did—that was the Flying Eagle way—but I'm so far down the bench I don't even have to go to most practices. And since no one expects me to play, least of all myself, I'm not all that emotionally involved. Still, at the end of rest hour, I change quickly into a Flying Eagle t-shirt, shorts and sneakers, grab my mitt, then haul up to the main yard just as a yellow school bus is pulling in front of the barn with the words HOLIDAY FARMS printed on the side in bold, black lettering. By that point, most of camp has joined the team to check out the opposition.

"What do you think?" Mateo asks me, drawing to my side.

He hadn't tried out for the team, probably because playing ball might have messed up his hair. "You guys have a chance?"

Given that Flying Eagle attracts kids on the artsier side, the answer is a clear no.

"Probably not," I say.

"I hear these Holiday Farms' kids are giants," Noah says, joining us. Today he's opted for his red high tops. "Total monsters. Mutants. Like out of science fiction."

I had heard the same thing. Tell the truth, the long-standing rivalry between the two camps isn't without its tensions. According to the rules the game is supposed to be for kids ages fourteen and under. But in years past, Flying Eagle suspected Holiday Farms of putting CITs (counselors in training) on the team. Totally unethical. Also unnecessary. Most camps could've beaten us with a group of five-year-olds.

"I do hear they're pretty large," I say.

"Who cares?" That's Oliver, of course. Hitting the pocket of his glove with his fist, he's ready for action. "Big or small, we're going to kick their butts."

With Oliver's words ringing through the air, the yellow bus hisses and the door swings open.

"Well," Mateo says. "Here they come."

Time to check out the enemy. Would they be too old? Too big? It doesn't take long to get an answer. That's because the first kid off the bus has a full-on goatee and the second has muscles that sprout mountains of other, even larger, muscles. Then comes kid number three, a broad-shouldered six-footer with a tattoo on his shoulder of a shark eating another shark.

Whispered objections fly up and down the Flying Eagle ranks.

"They're older'n my dad!"

"Darned supermen."

"Steroids, that's what they're on."

"Their steroids are on steroids!"

You might say that everyone is absolutely, positively full-on certain that Holiday Farms is cheating. Except Garth.

"I've read books about child development," he tells us. "Fourteen is a weird age. Some kids grow up fast."

"Get off it," Noah says. "Nobody grows up that fast."

Garth shrugs and lets it drop, but he's made his point. The rest of us look back at the three giants with new eyes. Is Garth right? Maybe. After all, I know full well that for every fourteen-year-old boy with a changed voice and a shaving kit there are two others still hovering at five feet, speaking higher than Elmo. And to tell the truth, after the three monsters get off the bus, the rest of the team looks more in keeping with the legal age limit—tiny, medium-sized, skinny and chubby kids—all wearing Holiday Farms t-shirts, all carrying baseball mitts. They must have sent their biggest kids off the bus first intentionally, just to intimidate us. It worked.

"Well, at least that's more like it," Oliver grunts.

Finally, the Holiday Farms coach appears, a twenty-something dude who's so impressively built he resembles an ultra-muscular cartoon character more than an actual human being. There's no one at Flying Eagle with that sort of physique—not even close.

"Hey, everyone!" His voice fills the main yard. "I'm Coach Timothy." He grins. "But you can call me Tank. Everyone at Holiday Farms does."

That's when our perfectly well-proportioned but normally built athletics head, Tad, steps forward to shake hands.

"Nice to meet you, Tank."

"You, too." Tank nods toward those of us in Flying Eagle t-shirts, holding mitts. "Are these your men?"

Tad can't hold back a smile. He's called us all sorts of names in practice, "boys, goons, idiots, book-wormed incompetents and iron-handed morons" but never men. Until now.

"That's right," he says, a little too forcefully. "My men." Then he turns to us. "Okay, then. Line it up!"

We had rehearsed this part. And I guess Holiday Farms had, too. Both teams line up then walk by the other, shaking hands. The kid with the goatee shakes mine so hard I worry about the

One Last Ride

long-term health of the bones in my pinky. Anyway, when the welcoming ritual is finished, Harvey Jones (the human version) appears, moving at a quick trot across the field, humming tunelessly. As usual, he's dressed in shorts, a yellow polo shirt, and hiking boots.

"Well, well, well. So it's Camp Holiday Farms! Welcome!"

Lou is right behind.

"Lou Hart," he says. "Assistant director."

As he and Tank shake hands, there's a second I think Lou is going to verbalize what every Flying Eagle camper and counselor is thinking, something along the lines of "Are you sure none of your players are in college?" Instead, Lou lets Tank's hand drop and says, "Nice to meet you." But Tank is no fool. He knows what everyone is thinking.

"I can assure you that all my men are of age," he announces. "I have their credentials on the bus."

Credentials? Did this guy come armed with birth certificates?

"No need," Harvey says, quickly. "Some boys just grow up fast."

"What I said," Garth whispers.

"Right," Lou says. "Let's get to the field."

Gametime.

Not quite yet. The door to the main house flies open and the eyes of over one hundred boys look up as Michelle steps into the sunshine, a ray of sunshine herself in a yellow blouse, cut-offs and flip-flops. Of course, we Flying Eagle boys are used to her. But the kids from Holiday Farms? They look at Michelle like a bunch of rabid dogs coming upon a slab of raw beef. That includes Tank. Suddenly, this very serious guy is beaming like one of those religious converts who hand out fliers in bus stations. And when Michelle approaches him, that smile gets even bigger.

"Sorry to be late," she says. "I'm Michelle, the nurse. I'll take care of things if any of your kids gets hurt during the game."

I swear that Tank's lip twitches—maybe he hasn't seen a woman as pretty as Michelle all summer? Maybe ever? Who knows?

"Hey, there," he says. "Coach Timothy."

I think it takes him a second to drop her hand. But I also think that I could see the wheels turning in his head, picturing some "alone" time with Michelle after game, maybe where she treats him for a pulled muscle back in her cabin. It's hard not to smile myself. Don't forget, I know what no one else knows: Tank, for all his muscles and rippling good looks, isn't her type. No, Michelle likes skinny weavers, not muscular supermen who name themselves after military equipment. Even so, I have a feeling that at that second, Coach Timothy's desire to destroy us on the field doubles. Sure, he wants to win for the boy's sake and the good name of Holiday Farms—but now he has a driving force: the love of a woman.

"All right, men," he says, finally dropping Michelle's hand. "To the field. March!"

"Right," Tad echoes. "March!"

So we march, the under-practiced, un-athletic crew of Flying Eagle athletes, leading the Holiday Farms team to Cowpatty field. As we round the dirt road to the pasture, the girls from RBG are already there, lined up and down the first and third base lines, ready to cheer us on. (Which is only fair because we had been forced to cheer for them in a round robin soccer tournament earlier that summer). Do I need to tell you that I immediately look for Luna? Of course I don't. But before I can locate her in the crowd, something else catches my eye: a horse, grazing ten feet behind second base, totally oblivious to the fact that he is standing smack in the middle of the field.

And that horse is Major!

Chapter 16

"An animal on the field?" Tank huffs.

"That's Major," Harvey Jones says. "He has a mind of his own."

"Does he now?" Tank says. "Well, so do I."

Clearly he's one of those gung-ho guys who takes control whether it's appropriate or not. No doubt: this is going to end badly.

"Hey, boy," Tank calls, clapping his hands. "Come on! Move it! We have a game to play!"

Major looks up from the grass, meets Tank's eyes, snorts, then goes back to grazing. I know from experience that once Major is settled in on a patch of good grass, there's no moving him. As for the other horses, they're about sixty feet away, still in centerfield, but so deep they're out of play. Even the kid with the shark tattoos probably can't hit it that far.

"Who's in charge of that animal?" Tank asks.

Harvey scans the crowd but I suspect that Scott has slipped off with Jeanne to the lower pasture. Doug is back in the cabin writing another sweet but terrible song for Courtney.

"Hmmm," Harvey says. "Our ranch counselors don't seem to be here at the moment."

The Tank smiles tightly. "We can hardly play baseball with a horse in short centerfield."

"Of course not," Harvey says. "We'll take care of this." He wheels around. "Greg Hill! Are you here? Greg?"

It's the logical move. After all, Greg is the best rider in camp and Scott's little brother. Like the members of Cabin Three, he's there to cheer us on.

"Here I am," Greg says, trotting over.

"See what you can do about moving Major into deep center," Harvey says.

Greg bites his lip.

"That horse doesn't like to be moved."

"I'll get him to move," a voice calls.

I turn. The kid with the goatee is marching forward.

"No, no," Harvey says, holding up his hand. "Let's solve this quietly. Greg. Do what you can. There's a good boy, thank you."

By that time, most of Flying Eagle has joined RBG up and down the first and third base lines. As both camps (and the Holiday Farms' players) look on, Greg walks through the infield, then stops on second base about ten feet from Major.

"Hey, boy!" he calls. "Come on. There's a game to play, okay?"

For those efforts, Major looks up from the grass and meets Greg's eyes with a hard stare. We can play around him for all he cares. Greg walks to Major's side and scratches him on the forehead. Major flicks his mane straight in Greg's face.

"Look at centerfield," Greg says, still not giving up. "Your buddies. Go hang with them."

One Last Ride

Even the prospect of peaceful afternoon with his pals and no campers on his back isn't going to move that horse from his afternoon snack. With a loud whinny he takes two steps forward and eats some more.

By this time, laughter is rippling through the RBG and Flying Eagle ranks. Even some kids on Holiday Farms are grinning.

"Unacceptable," Tank says. He nods at the kid with the goatee. "Do what you can, Ricky."

"Gotcha," Ricky says.

"Hold on here," Harvey says.

Ricky is already on the move. Opening his palm, he winds up. Then, before anyone can grab him, he swings hard at Major's rear. But the horse is too smart. At the last second, he sidesteps and Ricky lunges forward. All that's left now to finish the job is for Major to give him a little push with his forehead. Just like that, Ricky is toppling harmlessly to the outfield grass. The kids from Flying Eagle, RBG, and even Holidays Farms cheer.

"Lame, Ricky," the kid with the shark tattoos calls.

"Think you can do better, Otto?" Ricky replies as Tank helps him to his feet.

"I know I can," Otto replies.

"Do it then," Tank says.

"Hold on here!" Harvey calls.

But no way is a kid with shark tattoos on his bicep going to back down to a horse, no matter how large.

"Make room," he says.

"Stop!"

But the next thing I know, Otto is barreling toward Major all out. Then he's in the air. And what a leap! Bam! He lands smack on Major's back.

"Gotcha," he cries, steadying himself with the horse's mane. "Now yaaa!"

Not so fast. Major glances over his shoulder as though he's deciding whether or not to flick away a gnat, then bucks—not once—but three times, sending Otto somersaulting through the air. Seconds later, he lands hard on his butt.

"Ouch!" he calls. "Damn!"

That's when Michelle (who had been sitting next Jay Kreigel) comes running to see if she can help. And as she approaches, I can almost see the thought balloon forming over Tank's head. Now that his two strongest campers have failed, what better way to impress Flying Eagle's nurse than to demonstrate his own prowess with a particularly stubborn horse? Wouldn't it give them something else to talk about as she treats his muscle pull after the game?

"You all right?" she asks Otto.

"Oh, he's fine," Tank says.

"You sure?" Michelle asks.

"Yeah," Otto says, rising slowly to his feet. "I'm good."

"See?" Tank says. "My turn now."

"Hold on a second," Harvey says, not giving up. "Maybe we can play the game over at RBG?"

"No need for that," Tank says. "I've got this!"

"Man oh man," Joey says, drawing to my side. "This is going to be tyrannical."

Tyrannical isn't the right word but it's certainly going to be *something*. Maybe tragic. Because within seconds, over the continual objections of Harvey Jones, Tank is waving his arms like a windmill, hooting and hollering.

"Come on, boy! Move it, ya beast! Can't you see that we have a game to play?"

Clearly, Major does not see that. Another snort. More grass.

By now the crowd is riveted, watching to see the final showdown, man vs. horse.

Then the Holiday Farms kids begin to offer advice.

"Swat him on the rear, Tank!"

"Feed him a carrot!"

"Lead him by his teeth!"

But Tank has his own ideas. Grabbing the horse firmly by the mane, he yanks Major's head from the grass.

One Last Ride

"Perhaps we don't understand each other, sonny," he says with a frown. "We have a game."

Assuming that he has the upper hand, Tank pushes Major's head toward the outfield. Needless to say, Major is the one in control. Pushing right back, he shakes Tank off then trots to a new patch of grass by home plate and continues his feast.

"This is ridiculous," Tank calls.

"Jump on him!" a kid from Holiday Farms calls.

"Ride 'em, Tank!" another cries.

"Please," Harvey Jones calls. "These horses are insured for Flying Eagle campers only!"

It's too late. Just like that, Tank is sprinting even faster than Otto had before him. With a mighty leap, he's high in the air. But unlike Otto, Tank doesn't even make it to Major's back. At the last possible second, the horse lurches to the side then uses his powerful rump to bat Tank even further into the sky.

"Ahhhhh," Tank calls.

Splat! He belly flops directly onto home plate.

But even then, Major isn't done. Clearly, this is a horse who is sick and tired of having his afternoon snack interrupted. The second Tank lands, Major bites hard onto his collar and begins to trot briskly backwards, dragging him up the first base line!

"Stop!" Tank calls, bumping up and down on his stomach. "I said stop!"

But Major won't stop.

"Lookit," a kid from Holiday Farms calls. "He's rounding first."

It's true! Apparently, Major has paid closer attention during softball practice than anyone could've imagined. His goal soon becomes clear: to drag Tank around *all* the bases!

Suddenly everyone is cheering and yelling at once.

"He's on second!"

"He's rounding third!"

"Stop!" Tank calls.

"He's gonna score!"

Which is when Major slides Tank across home, leaving the

Holiday Farms' coach lying on the plate with a mouthful of dirt. As Major trots back toward the pitching mound to resume grazing, gales of laughter rip across the field.

"Oh, my goodness," Michelle says, kneeling by Tank's side. "Are you okay?"

Clearly too embarrassed to even enjoy a quick exam by the beautiful nurse, Tank wobbles to his feet and faces Harvey Jones. "What now? Will my players have to dodge a horse all afternoon?"

Which is when I suddenly know what to do. Without saying a word, I begin to jog past Major to the deep outfield.

"Where are you going, Jackson?" Harvey calls.

"I have an idea," I call then keep jogging.

True, my previous attempt at bareback had ended in disaster, but what other choice do I have? Who is the only being on planet earth who could get Major to move? Merrylegs.

"Come on, girl," I say when I reach her. "Nice and easy."

I hoist myself as gently as I can onto her back, then hold on loosely to her mane. Merrylegs knows what to do. She walks—not trots, Thank God—across the field to Major's side. Then I keep her walking and, as I hoped, like magic, Major decides that there's more to life than food. As the kids from RBG, Flying Eagle, and even Holiday Farms cheer (and Tank, Ricky and Otto look on aghast), I circle the infield once, then lead Major back to the deep outfield, almost to the border of the pine forest. Then I finally hop off and come running back across the outfield as all the kids rise as one, applauding like mad. Flying Eagle kids are cheering most loudly of all. Can you blame them? Don't forget, we're all but certain to get our butts kicked in the game. Getting Major to move after the trio from Holiday Farms tried and failed is a victory unto itself: probably the only one we'll get that day.

"All right," Tad calls. "Let's play some ball already!"

Chapter 17

I guess there are times in life when a guy has to cede to stage. Sure, I had saved the day with Major, but when it came to the game itself, it was all Oliver. I don't know if I've ever witnessed an athletic performance so great. I've seen some pro athletes do some pretty amazing things, but that's on TV. This was up close, in real life. A kid from my very own cabin. So what if he was an obnoxious idiot with a foul mouth? Sometimes you've got to give credit where it's due. Oliver was the smallest guy on the field, but also the best.

It starts in the first inning when Holiday Farms tees up on our pitcher, a lanky Cabin Nine kid named Phil Finglehopper (that's his actual name) and scores four quick runs. But the Flying Eagles come charging back in the bottom of the first, loading the bases on two walks and a weak single. Then Oliver hits a screamer over the third basemen's head that the left fielder loses by the gate to Trudi's pen. When the dust clears, Oliver is standing on third with a three-run triple.

After that, the game is closer than we ever would have imagined—and again all because of Oliver. He gets his hits, of course—a single, then a double, then another single—but mostly it's his play at shortstop that keeps us close. The kid is everywhere, diving on grounders, making laser sharp throws, hurling himself onto the outfield grass to catch pop-ups. In the fourth inning, he turns an unassisted double-play. In the sixth he catches a line drive then doubles a Holiday Farms batter off of first. In the seventh, he flies out of nowhere to spear another liner.

All of which results in a miracle—a game where the Flying Eagles should've been creamed is close, going into the bottom of the eighth! And then? When Oliver gets his fourth hit of the day, another double, this one to right center, we go up by two runs! Which means that headed into the top of the ninth the score is Flying Eagle 11 - Holiday Farms 9.

As for me, I'm perfectly happy to spend the entire day at the end of the bench where I belong. Sure, I feel a little bit jealous at Oliver's wild success. After all, Luna is there watching him—I had finally spotted her, kneeling up the third base line—and even though she's stood me up I still like her. What if Oliver uses this amazing performance to get her back? On the other hand, who cares? At that moment, all of Oliver's bragging is forgiven. He's the game's hero.

But then it happens—my safe little world at the far end of the bench crumbles. I first get a bad feeling when Harvey Jones wanders over to whisper something in Tad's ear. That bad feeling turns to panic when Tad looks down the bench and nods, with a sigh. Because I know what's about to go down. Moments later, the starters begin to get pulled to give the bench-warmers a chance to play. It's the Flying Eagle way: participation means more than victory. Pretty dumb, if you ask me. I mean, I want to win.

One Last Ride

Anyway, one by one, in go the subs, those of us who either don't like softball much or who like it but aren't very good. I'm the only one left on the bench, but not for long, because soon enough, Tad taps my shoulder.

"Second base, Jackson."

Even though I saw what had been happening, I can't quite believe that I'm going to get in the game, too. Not only am I one of the youngest on the team, I'm one of the least talented. Grabbing my mitt, I jog nervously onto the field. Cheers rise from the sidelines, mostly from the kids from Cabin Three.

"Go, Jackson!" Mateo calls.

"Do it for Harvey Jones!" Noah says, clearly referring to our chipmunk.

Garth is reading and doesn't say a word. But Oliver has a thing or two to say. Still at shortstop—Tad is no fool, he's not going to take out his best player—Oliver glares at me.

"Try not to screw up, okay?"

I swallow hard. "Okay."

The next play I screw up. With one out and a runner on first, the Goatee Man hits a hard grounder to Oliver which he fields cleanly. I get over to second to cover at least. But when Oliver flips me the ball I drop it and the Holiday Farms runner is safe. Oliver shoots me a killer look and returns to his position, probably realizing that he's going to have to win this game on his own. The next hitter gets a double, driving in the runner from second, making the score 11 to 10. The hitter after that singles, then moves up a base on an error, putting runners on second and third. But the hitter after that pops up to third base. Now there are two outs. But here's the bad news: stepping up to the plate is none other than Otto, the Shark Tattoo Man, walloper of two massive homeruns, one that flies clear over the left field fence into the pig sty.

"Play back!" Ted calls from the bench.

I do as I'm told. As Otto steps into the batter's box, the kids on the sidelines are mostly standing now, some cheering, some nervously biting their nails, some even closing their eyes.

When Phil winds up, I can hear my heart pounding in my throat.

"Hit it to Oliver," I whisper. "Oliver!"

Really, I don't care where he hits it, as long as it isn't to me.

Phil throws a fast one.

"Strike one!" the ump calls.

Otto had swung and missed! But that only makes him look more determined. I swear, he clenches the bat like it's one of those little souvenirs sold in ballparks. I glance nervously around the field. There's my cabin: Mateo, Garth, and Noah. And then I see Luna, leaning forward, looking my way!

The next pitch is a ball. As our catcher throws Phil back the ball, I blink and refocus.

"Get your eyes off of Luna," Oliver snaps.

"What?" I say.

Was I that obvious?

"You heard me. Look alive! This kid hit it to right field two times."

I nod. "Got it!"

A lie. I don't have it at all. I'm shaking like I'm plugged into an electrical outlet. There's nowhere to hide. And then Phil nods to the catcher…he winds up…he throws a pitch that catches the outside corner of the plate…

Otto swings!

Crack!

As the runners on second and third begin to run, the ball rockets high in the air—directly over second base!

I look up. The ball is mine! But then…disaster! I can't see the darned thing! The sun is in my eyes! I run wildly to my right, then back to my left, then I blink again and like a miracle there it is, revolving like a moon. I back up. Then I run forward, my mitt over my head.

"Catch it!" the first baseman cries.

What does he think I'm trying to do?

"Back!" Oliver calls. "Give him room!"

I've misjudged it! The ball is falling fast, dropping behind me! I'm going to miss it. I run backward, sprinting madly, mitt outstretched behind me. Then suddenly, I'm slipping—on what I don't know—then I'm slipping faster, then falling backwards, and then—plop! I'm on my back and the ball is in my mitt!

I've caught it!

"Out!" the ump calls.

I hold the ball over my head. The Flying Eagle and RBG sides break into wild applause. I look to Luna. She's beaming. The first baseman gives me a hug and then I'm swarmed by the entire team, hugging me, slapping my back, telling me "Way to Go!" But by then I can smell it. Oliver is the first to push me away and laugh. In seconds, everyone is cracking up. The Flying Eagle softball field isn't called Cowpatty field for nothing, right? Sure, Tad had done his best to clear all the horse and cow manure off the field before the game. Apparently, there was one he had missed. Leave it to me to step in it. Then again, isn't that what causes me to slip backwards and catch the ball?

"That's what I call a home field advantage," Noah yells, running toward me.

By that point, I see the cow dung all over my sneakers and calves.

"Someone clean this kid!" Phil Finklehopper yells.

On cue, someone dumps a bucket of bug juice on my head. Now I'm filthy and sticky. Then Mateo is at my side, holding out his I-phone.

"I gotta have this," he says. "Lemme get a picture."

Do I have a choice? Mateo snaps it. Then to make matters worse, as the team clears away to celebrate with other friends—and to get away from me—Florence is suddenly by my side. She has a way of just showing up.

"Wow," she says. "Nice catch!"

"Thanks!" I say.

"Is that really cow dung on your sneakers? And your legs? And your...shirt?"

My shirt!?

"Interesting," Florence says. "At first, I thought it might have been from a horse."

"Nope," Garth says, walking up. "It was cow dung. I could tell by how Jackson slipped."

"What?" Florence says. "From the angle he fell?"

"Exactly," Garth says.

"Whatever," I say—the last thing I want is to hear Florence and Garth debate my manure plunge. Despite being covered I'm already scanning the crowd for Luna. To my horror, she's talking to Oliver! Or trying to—the kid is surrounded, by half of RBG, including Emma, not letting any other girl get too close. Not that Oliver doesn't deserve it. He's the camp hero, after all. Even I'm partly in awe of him.

"Okay, Ruth Bader Ginsberg!" Mrs. Davenport calls, ringing a cowbell. "Back to camp! Back to camp!"

Wouldn't you know it? That's when Luna finally catches my eye.

"Hey!" she calls over. "Great catch!"

"Yeah," I call back. "Thanks."

Has she seen what I have slipped in? I can't be sure. But to my surprise, she starts my way.

"Don't stress about it," she says, indicating my dirty sneakers. "I was shoveling stalls the other day and slipped in a whole pile of it."

"Really?"

"Really."

Mrs. Davenport rings her bell again. The RBG kids begin to walk slowly back across the pasture.

"I guess you'd better go, right?"

To my surprise, she doesn't move. Then she unleashes a shocker.

"Wanna walk me back?"

I blink.

"To RBG?"

"Yeah," she says. Then a more serious look passes her face. "There's something I wanted to talk about. Actually, have you ever been to the spring where the horses drink?"

It's deep in the pine forest. Where is this girl taking me? What does she want?

"Yeah, I've been there. Once."

"There's a bucket there. You can wash off your sneakers."

With that, she turns and starts walking. What do I do? The two ball teams are headed back to the main yard for popsicles. But some things are more important than dessert. With a quick look to make sure no one is looking, I jog behind.

Chapter 18

At first Luna and I make chit-chat about the game, but then we walk in silence through the pine forest, as if by some unspoken understanding that she'll tell me what she wants to talk about once we reach the spring. That's fine by me. With my shirt still soaked with bug juice and cow dung on my sneakers, it's hard to make conversation anyway. Soon enough we see a clearing in the distance.

"There it is," Luna says.

A moment later, she's filling one of the buckets with water.

"Hey, take off your shoes."

I do as I'm told and Luna dumps some water onto my dirty sneakers. Then I wet down some leaves and wipe off my legs. It isn't totally clean—not by a longshot—but it is better. By that point, Luna is seated on a large rock by the spring.

"Wow," I say, finally. Someone has to speak, right? "I can't believe Tad put me in the game. I stunk so badly out there."

Luna seems surprised. "Um, you made the game winning catch."

"Before that," I repeat. "I didn't know what I was doing out there. You saw my error."

"Okay," she says. "But like I said, after that, the catch."

She's trying to be supportive, I know that, but I feel slightly annoyed anyway. Mostly because I'm nervous. Being alone with a girl in the woods is a new thing. And what does Luna want to talk about anyway? Is she going to break up with me even though we aren't even going out? Apparently not.

"You also got on Merrylegs bareback with no bridle," she goes on. "Didn't you tell me you just started riding this summer?"

I don't let on—or I try not to show it—but that little comment makes me feel better. A lot better, especially after falling off and rupturing myself the day before.

"Yeah," I say. "This summer." I can't resist putting myself down. I do that sometimes. Not sure why. "But I still suck at softball."

Luna comes back with the perfect answer.

"Softball is overrated." She nods back up the forest toward the field. "Not to mention some of the players. You should've heard Oliver going off a minute ago. I swear, that kid is his own best fan club."

I smiled full-out at that. Can you blame me? She had paid me a compliment and trashed Oliver.

"He does brag a lot."

Luna laughs. "You think? He said we could call him Shohei Ohtani if we wanted. That's when I left."

It's incredible what a little moral support and put-down of a rival can do for a kid's state of mind. Suddenly, I like this girl again. Maybe even love her. Then I see that day's t-shirt. "EAT ORGANIC!" I have to sit next to her on the rock to keep from passing out.

"So listen," Luna says.

"What?"

Finally, the big moment has arrived. Luna pauses, as though looking for the right words. I have no idea what's coming but I know what I want to hear: her confessing her undying love for me. Or maybe she's going to apologize again for standing me up at the costume cabin—that would be enough. Instead, I get another curveball.

"I hope it's okay to say this, but my mom told me about your parents."

I swallow hard. I know word spreads quickly at Flying Eagle, but I didn't realize gossip went across the pasture so fast.

"Really?"

Luna nods. "She didn't mean any harm. She wanted me to know."

"What did she tell you?"

"That you don't know who's picking you up or where you'll be living."

"Oh, yeah," I mutter. "That."

I almost ask if her mother had told her how I had cried for an hour, but I decide to keep quiet.

"My parents split up for six months a couple of years ago."

I'm stunned. I mean, this is huge. Lou and Amanda? They are the happiest couple in the solar system. Down to earth, kind, a history teacher (him) and a guidance counselor (her), they're perfect. If Lou and Amanda have separated, even briefly, how is love even possible?

"You're kidding. Why?"

"They never told me exactly, but Dad moved out for the second half of fifth grade. Then after he and I came up here for the summer, they patched things up in the fall and it's been fine ever since. At least, it seems fine. So what I'm saying is you never know."

I still don't feel optimistic about my own parents. But it feels nice to hear about a couple that find a way back to each other.

"I didn't know if I should tell you," Luna says. "I didn't want to get too personal."

"No, no, I'm glad you did."

I want to say more but can't think of a single thing out of the million in my head. Until I suddenly know exactly what I want to ask. It's a risk but isn't this turning into one of those "let's be honest with each other" conversations?

"So listen," I begin, haltingly.

That's as far as I get. As usual, Luna is miles ahead of me.

"You want to know what happened the other night? When I stood you up?"

This girl is psychic. "Were you really scared of your dad finding you?"

"That." She pauses. "And...I got nervous, I guess."

The woods suddenly never felt so still.

"About...*me*?"

It's sort of hard to believe.

"Yeah." She sort of whispers it then gives me a playful kick. "About meeting a *boy*. And to tell the truth, Mateo and Patti are taking things kind of fast." She looks me square in the eye. "I don't know about you, but I've never kissed anyone before."

Boy, this girl is honest! All the stuff I keep to myself or feel embarrassed about, she blurts right out.

"Me neither," I say.

Actually, I practically shout it. Then we both smile like we've won the lottery or something. Total relief.

"Really?" she says.

"Really."

"Because I just want the first one to be with a nice guy, you know?"

"Yeah, me, too. But you know, a nice girl."

Did I really say that? Because wham! Suddenly, the pressure is back on. It seems pretty clear, right? I'm the nice guy that she wants to kiss! The question is if she wants to do it right then? I mean, what better place for a first kiss than by a spring in a pine forest?

One Last Ride

The trouble is that I have no idea whatsoever how to proceed. For starters, how does a boy tell for absolute certain if a girl even wants to be kissed? Does she part her lips? Paint a sign on her forehead? Scream "Kiss me, already!" in my face? Or do I forget about her signs and follow my instincts? But how do I even know what those are? Don't some instincts have to be taught? Sure, my dad had told me the facts of life, but no one had ever told me how to lean quietly forward and place my lips on a girl's.

I look at Luna again. Is she waiting for me to act? I can't really tell...but if she is...what do I do?

Then it hits me: I *ask*.

"Hey, Luna."

This is hard.

"Yeah?" she says.

I don't know if I'll be able to get out the next few words. But then, I'm off the hook. See, there's a distant tromping in the woods. We both look toward the noise, then as the tromping gets louder, Luna stands up.

"What's that?"

For a second I think of Scott and Jeanne the other day in the pasture. Maybe it's them right now, coming to hang by the spring, too? Instead, Rusty breaks into the clearing, holding hands with his third—yes *third*—girlfriend of the summer, Sami, the pottery counselor from RBG. Mateo's right. During the last week of camp, staff sneak around as much as campers.

"Well, well," Rusty says. "Look! It's Jackson and the assistant director's daughter!"

Luna looks mortified. "Oh, God! Don't tell my parents."

"Yeah, please!" I say.

Rusty? He milks the moment just like I guessed he might.

"I don't know," he says to Sami as he fiddles with his sideburns. He likes to do that, as if reminding himself how cool he is to have them. "Should we turn them in?"

Sami smiles. "Nah, let's let them off the hook."

"Wow, thanks," I say.

Luna nods. "That goes double for me."

"But we do need to get back to camp," Rusty says. "All of us. Almost dinnertime."

"Yeah," I say. "Sure."

Luna shoots me a look. I think we're both relieved.

"See you at the fair then?" she says. "Or maybe the musical?"

"Absolutely," I say.

She flashes me that big gummy smile. I have to admit it—I sort of swoon. Maybe we'll live to kiss another day? Maybe not. But right then, that smile is enough.

"Okay, bye then."

"Yeah, bye."

Moments later, Sami and Luna disappear into the pine forest and Rusty and I mosey back toward Flying Eagle.

"Nice girl," he says.

"Yeah."

Rusty waits for me to say something more, I think, but I keep my mouth shut. After all, what *can* I say? That I was close to my first kiss but he screwed it up? That isn't the truth anyway. The truth is that I couldn't tell if the moment was right then I waited too long to ask. Anyway, before long we reach Cowpatty Field, now deserted but for the horses and Trudi. Major is where I expected, standing next to Merrylegs. Copper is nearby, looking on.

"Hey, nice catch by the way," Rusty says. "Way to win the game."

"It was lucky."

"Maybe a little," Rusty says with a laugh. "But I couldn't have caught it. No way. You did all right."

"Thanks," I say.

Then I can't resist. I mean, Rusty is on what...girlfriend number three?

"So you and Sami?"

Rusty shrugs. "Yeah, for now, anyway."

Man oh man, I envy him—to be that relaxed about girls. I

can't conceive of it.

"So I don't mean to pry," Rusty says.

"That's okay," I say.

"Well, you and Luna...I hope Sami and I didn't interrupt."

I know what he means but I'm too embarrassed to answer directly. Instead, I stare straight ahead, praying Rusty won't see how I'm blushing. Finally, I shake my head.

"Nah. You didn't. Nothing happened." Then I just say it: "Sometimes I wonder if I'll ever kiss a girl."

Rusty stops and fingers those sideburns of his. "Try not to worry about that." He says it pretty gently for him. "You'll get there. Wait for the right moment."

Easy for him to say, right? The right moment? When? At the fair? When I'm in college? At that moment, the idea of a single kiss seems as distant as a weekend tour of the Andromeda Galaxy.

But then something sweet happens. To my surprise, Rusty puts an arm around my shoulder and gives me a squeeze.

"You'll get there," he repeats.

"I will?"

He nods. "You may not know it yet. But I do."

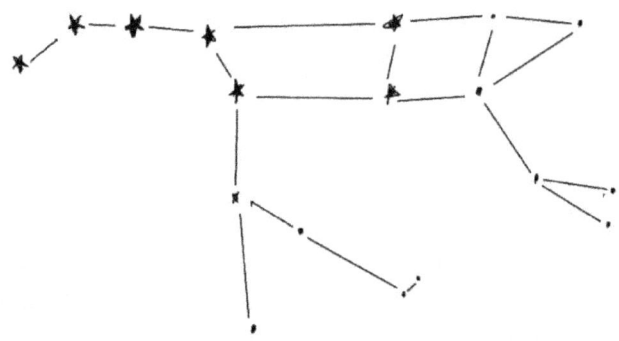

Chapter 19

About once a week, Harvey checks the weather report for clear skies, then lets whoever wants to drag their sleeping bag outside to sleep under the stars. Though campers are given permission to mix and match, Cabin 3 usually sticks together—by that point in the summer, for better or worse, we're a unit. That night we camp only thirty or so feet from our cabin, but under the vastness of the Vermont sky, it feels like the middle of nowhere. The stars are beautiful, shining brilliantly.

We've just settled in our sleeping bags, with flashlights, books, pillows, and the remains of a box of chocolate chip cookies Mateo's stolen from the kitchen, when Oliver
   gets right to it—talking about himself, of course. And why

not? It's all he's talked about during dinner, too. And yeah, he had been good in the game—amazing—but enough is enough. So Noah shines his flashlight into the sky.

"Yo, check that out," he says. "The Big Dipper."

I had seen it the minute we had lay down. We all had. The Big Dipper is hard to miss even for a city kid.

"Yo," Oliver says. "We were talking about the game."

"Not anymore," Garth says. "And look! There's the Little Dipper."

I had seen that, too, just about the extent of my knowledge of the solar system.

Noah directs his flashlight at another group of stars. "Look there! That's the constellation that makes up the bear."

"What bear?" Oliver asks, giving in to the change of topic. Maybe even he is finally sick of talking about himself.

"You know, the bear. I forget the name."

"Which stars do you mean?" Mateo asks.

Noah points again, using his flashlight to point them out. "That one, that one, that one, that one, that one, and that one."

Mateo laughs. "There are literally billions of stars up there. How are we supposed to know which ones you're pointing at?"

"I'm shining my flashlight."

"Your flashlight goes maybe fifty feet into the dark! The stars are like a million light years away!"

"Garth knows where I'm pointing, don't you Garth?"

"Sort of," Garth replies. "But that's no bear."

"Sure it is," Noah says. "I read a book about it once."

"Sorry," Mateo says. "But those stars don't look like a bear to me either."

"Then what?" Noah says.

"That's easy," Oliver says. He gives Noah a whack. "Your fat belly."

Yep, Oliver could be a real sweetheart.

"Hey, weight shaming is totally uncool," Mateo says. "Besides, we're talking about the stars not body parts."

"Stars are boring," Oliver says. "I mean, they're pretty, I get that. But what is there to say about them? Nothing. New subject, okay?"

"I've got one then," Mateo says.

I have a feeling what's coming. See, that evening I told him every gory detail of my walk to the spring with Luna. Of course, he had told everyone else.

"Jackson had a good afternoon," my friend goes on.

"I know it," Garth says. "Great catch."

Mateo laughs. "I'm not talking about the catch."

Oliver takes the bait, of course.

"I still can't believe Luna asked you to go to the spring."

"Why not?" Noah says. "She likes him."

"Hard to believe," Oliver snickers.

"Shut up," I say.

"What he said," Mateo says. "Shut up. What matters is what comes next. Jackson is going to take her into the nature room at the fair, get under that table and kiss her."

Oliver laughs. "Because if he doesn't, I will!"

"What?" I say. Suddenly, I feel super possessive. I mean, Luna doesn't even like him anymore. "What about Emma?"

"She's still in the picture. I'll make out with them both."

"Dream on," Mateo says. "Luna's going to make out with Jackson."

"Not just make out," Noah says with a laugh. "They're going to *make love*!"

We all gasp.

"Make love?" Oliver hoots. "Did you just say that?"

Noah shrugs. "Isn't that what grown-ups call it?"

"We're twelve," Mateo reminds him.

"I'd be happy enough to just hold someone's hand," Garth says quietly.

I'm surprised. I didn't think Garth liked girls at all. Things change fast.

"So maybe you'll find someone at the fair, too," Mateo says. Then he nudges Noah. "Maybe you, as well."

Noah shakes his head firmly. "Don't think so. My feelings haven't changed since the summer began."

"What?" Mateo says. "Gay but currently inactive?"

Noah nods. "Exactly."

"I hear you," Mateo says. He pauses then goes for it. "But maybe it's time to get in the game. There's gotta be somebody here you sort of like."

If it wasn't so dark, I have a strong feeling we'd see Noah blushing. Maybe Mateo is right? Maybe there is someone? We never get a chance to find out. Suddenly, Doug is standing there. We haven't even heard him walk up.

"Hey, boys."

Obviously, he's heard the last minute of conversation—I mean, how can he have missed it? Farmers in nearby Gainesville were probably calling camp to beg us to shut up. Even so, we aren't embarrassed—not in front of Doug.

"You know," he says, sitting down. "You all have plenty of time for kissing and everything else. No rush. Sorry to break up the party. I'm just dropping by to tell you guys that I spoke to Harvey. We've got the horses tomorrow for hike day."

I'm surprised. Most cabins go on actual hikes under the power of their own feet. Though Doug has threatened to use his position at the ranch to take the horses all summer I never expected him to go through with it. As far as I know, Noah and Oliver have only been on a horse once or twice in their entire lives.

"I can't ride a horse," Oliver says.

My thoughts exactly.

"Sure you can," Doug replies, calmly. "Jackson and I will show you how."

Again, I'm happy for the cover of darkness. Another blush, this one out of pride.

"It'll be fun," Doug goes on. "We'll take it easy, okay?"

"Take it easy?" Noah says. "If I go, I wanna gallop."

Doug laughs. "If we gallop, you'll fall off on your butt."

He stands back up.

"Anyway, I didn't mean to get in the way of your conversation." He pauses. "I believe the subject was kissing, right?"

"Right," Noah says.

"Have fun," Doug says.

With that, he's gone, swallowed up in the darkness.

"Cool," Mateo says. "Horses."

"Yeah, should be fun," I say.

The minute the words are out of my mouth, I have a worry: which kid will ride which horse? Obviously, Doug will take Major. Would that leave me with Copper? Or would Doug give him to Rusty? I really don't know. The rest of the horses are easy enough. One thing for certain: I'm not getting Merrylegs. A mount that easy has to be saved for one of the beginners.

"Listen up, guys," Noah says, leaning on his elbow. "I've got a game."

"A game?" Oliver says.

"Yeah, a fun one." Noah sits up. "Some friends and I played it on a sleep over at home. We go in a circle, right? And each of us tells a line in a story."

"I hate telling stories," Oliver says. "What's so great about that?"

"Not just any story," Noah goes on. "A sexy story about someone here—with lots of details."

"This is sounding better," Mateo says. "How about Jackson and Luna?"

I could've guessed that was coming.

"Oh, come on!"

"No, that's good," Garth says. "I know exactly where we can set it—in *Rivendell*."

"*Rivendell*?" Oliver says. "Where is that?"

"It's the elf kingdom," Garth says. "*The Lord of the Rings*, guys!"

Which is when the second visitors of the night appear. If someone had given me a gun I might have used it—on myself. Lou and Amanda emerge out of the darkness.

"Hey, fellas," Lou says. "Time to keep it down. Try and go to sleep."

As usual, the only sign that he's heard any of our conversation is the slight smile that curves under his mustache.

"Sure thing," Noah says.

"Yeah," Garth says. "Sorry, Lou."

"No problem," Oliver says.

"Okay," I manage.

I look up from my sleeping bag. Lou is already walking off, now holding hands with Amanda. Had they heard the guys suggesting they make up a story about me and their daughter? Probably. Most fathers would've strung me up by then. But watching Lou and Amanda disappear into the darkness I think about something else: what Luna had told me. It seems impossible to believe that they had separated. They seem way too close. Had they once been as miserable as my parents? Had Amanda wandered their house in tears? Had Lou looked into the distance during dinner, like he wished he was on another planet? How did they find their way back to one another? Could my parents pull off the same trick? Would they be happily holding hands a couple of years down the line?

"What're you thinking?"

That's Mateo. Garth and Oliver are now reading in their sleeping bags with flashlights. And Noah? The guy is already dozing off.

"Nothing," I say to Mateo. "You?"

"Nothing," Mateo replies.

Two bigger liars have never lived. We're thinking about everything all at once with as many thoughts as there are stars in the sky.

"Hey, Jackson."

"What?"

"I was thinking. At the fair. While you kiss Luna, I might go for second base with Patti."

This is news, worthy of rising back up to my elbow.

"Whoa, really? Like feel her up? Underneath her shirt?"

He shakes his head. "Just over and only if I get the guts."

"Incredible," I say.

"But you have to go for that kiss," Mateo replies.

"I'm not even sure she likes me."

"She likes you, you fool."

"You don't think she still likes Oliver—maybe just a little bit?"

"Oliver? She hates him. That's what she told you, right?"

"She said he was bragging."

"See? She likes you, okay?"

"Thanks, man."

"Sure thing."

I think we both want the conversation to continue. But we have both reached that point where staying awake takes all our energy. So I lay back down and look overhead. Faced with the hugeness of the sky, my problems suddenly feel very small. Who cares what happens with Luna? Or my parents even? Or what horse I get assigned on the trail ride? Who cares about anything? Then to further highlight my total cosmic nothingness another shooting star rockets across the sky.

"Hey," I manage. "See that?"

Mateo doesn't reply. I glance over. He's on his side, asleep.

A minute later, I am, too.

Chapter 20

That morning, I wake to the sight of kids gathered around the center of the row, laughing. At first, I'm too groggy to know what I'm looking at. But it becomes clear before long: someone—probably Oliver though he denies it—has taken all three pairs of Noah's high tops, tied them to a string and hoisted them up the flagpole!

Noah takes it in stride—what other choice does he have with everyone gathered around laughing? But I can tell he's pissed, especially when one of the red ones comes down with a big smudge mark on it. I mean, his high tops are his security blanket. I think that bothers him more than being called overweight.

"Whoever did this I would like to kill," Noah announces at

breakfast. "I mean, literally destroy."

We all look to Oliver, even Doug and Rusty.

"What?" he says. "I didn't touch his frigging sneakers."

No one believes him but with no proof what can we do?

Anyway, an even bigger surprise than the sight of Noah's beloved high tops dangling in the breeze lies in store for me that morning. Doug breaks the news on the way to the ranch after the first activity bell.

"Take a deep breath," he begins.

This doesn't sound good.

"Why?"

"I've decided to lead the cabin trailride on Copper," he says. "You'll take Major and ride about halfway down the line behind Merrylegs."

I'm stunned. I've simply assumed that Doug, the best rider, will take Major, the most difficult horse.

"What?"

"You heard me."

"Are you sure? I can't do that."

"Sure you can." Doug gets down on one knee to explain his reasoning. "I have to lead, right? And Major doesn't do well out in front. He's too strong. It'd be hard for even me to keep him going slow enough. Remember, we've got a lot of beginners on this ride."

"I know," I say. "But what if Major causes trouble?"

"He won't," Doug says. "You rode him well in the ring."

Untrue!

"He bucked me off! I nearly died!"

"Only when you were cantering," Doug says. "When you were walking the ring you were great. And don't forget, you're going to be behind Merrylegs, right? Major will be thrilled to stay right where he is. Just keep him on her butt and it'll all work out."

I know better than to argue with Doug. When we get to the ranch, he assigns the rest of the horses. The line stacks up like this: Doug up front on Copper; Mateo next on Strawberry;

One Last Ride

Garth, the lucky jerk, on Merrylegs; then me on Major, followed by Noah on Echo; Oliver on sweaty Blondie, and Rusty bringing up the rear on old-man Gidget.

Despite my doubts, Doug's strategy works. Yep, my other cabinmates are horseback riding disasters. They hold the reins too loosely. They slouch. Noah and Oliver kick Echo and Blondie so hard I think they'll draw blood. But despite Major and Copper's power and Blondie's sweat, these are well-trained animals, used to carrying inexperienced kids on their backs. Put them in a line and they generally stay the course.

So the morning passes more happily than I expect. Doug leads us on a windy route through the back woods of camp, across fields, by a stone fence or two, through the nooks and crannies of the countryside. And hand and hand with the standard Vermont scenery comes the standard boy-talk. Girls, sports, science fiction, kids in other cabins (the weird ones), and finally, the disgustingness of the camp ravioli—we talk about it all. There are also moments of peace, too, times when everyone, Oliver included, gets lost in his thoughts, or simply enjoys the beauty of the surroundings. By the time we stop for lunch, on a shady field (part of the massive camp property but a good three miles from the main house), everyone in the cabin seems sold on riding.

"This is so danged easy," Oliver declares. "I mean, if I knew how easy horseback riding was, I would've come to the ranch now and then."

No way I'm going to let someone like Oliver put down what I had accomplished that summer.

"We've been walking and you're on Blondie," I say. "An eight-year-old could handle him."

Oliver shrugs. Maybe even he gets that I'm right? Anyway, with the horses tied to trees in the shade, we break out the PB&J and juice and cookies. After clean-up, Rusty lies back with a hat over his eyes and takes a short nap, while the rest of us explore a nearby creek. Noah tries to catch a frog and gets a foot soaked. Soon enough, it's time for Act Two of our expedition. Clearly, Doug feels good about how we've handled the morning, because after ten minutes on a winding dirt path, he opens things up to a trot.

"Keep the reins short and squeeze hard with your legs," he calls back. "Keep your butts in the saddle."

I'm probably as nervous as anyone when we go to the faster gait. The last thing I want is for Major to go crazy. But after a few steps, I relax. As long as I keep him behind Merrylegs, he's on automatic pilot. All I have to do is sit and make sure I don't fall off. When we hit a narrow dirt road Doug allows the horses to stretch the trot to a canter. Whoops and hollers filled the air.

"Yee-haw!"

"Ex-cell-ent!"

"Damn, I'm good!"

"Nah, you suck. *I'm* good!"

"I'm the one who's good!"

"Shut up! We're *all* good!"

With that point settled, we ride on.

"Okay, boys," Doug calls, as we reach a small field. "Let's take it easy for a while."

Before long, the horses are catching their breath and nibbling at the long grass and timothy. On one side of the field are two oak trees. But on the far side is another path that leads up a steep hill. That's when I realize where we are. Up the path is the Antique Road, a mile long straight-away, almost entirely unused by cars, where the older kids bring the horses to run. Greg, Barry, and Joey have all galloped there. I hadn't but I was hoping.

The trouble is this: the Antique Road has an almost chemical effect on the horses. After a quick munch at the grass, even the slow ones—Echo and Gidget—begin to sidestep and pull toward the incline, recognizing exactly where they are: the place they are usually brought to sprint all out. How should they know that that wasn't on the agenda for that afternoon?

Raring to go, Copper whirls in a circle. Doug stays on easily, holding a short rein.

"Whoa, there, buddy."

He turns back to the group and tells everyone what I already knew.

"Let's move on in the other direction and they'll calm down."

"Good," Oliver says. "This horse is sweating like a pig."

I glance over my shoulder. Blondie is hot and bothered, even by his wet standards.

"Okay, everyone," Doug says. "Just follow me."

No sooner are the words out of Doug's mouth than Copper turns in another sharp circle and snorts. A morning of walking and one light canter has left him itching for more. The horse wants to run. Major, too. I think I have him under control, but he suddenly rears so abruptly it's a minor miracle I don't fall off. Then as soon as all four of his feet are planted, he pulls like a madman for the incline. Meanwhile, Copper is still giving Doug a hard time, prancing in place and snorting. Are these two horses aiming for another showdown, perhaps the final one of the summer? Is Major still smarting over his loss to Copper in the pasture? Looks that way.

"Short rein, Jackson," Doug calls back to me.

I don't have to be told. I'm pulling with all my life.

"Come on, boy," I say. "Back in line."

For a second it seems to work. Somehow I get Major's face pointed at Merryleg's butt, his dream position. But his raw desire to put Copper back in his place is too strong. When he side-steps again I can't control him.

"Hey!" I call.

As Doug fights Copper to a standstill, Major lunges for the road. For a second he's in total control, racing up the incline. Then I give it one last shot, pulling back on the reins as hard as I can. Major rears again. When he comes down, I yank him around, away from the road, facing the other horses.

"Nice!" Rusty calls.

Major isn't done. He rears again, rising so high that we

stand at a ninety-degree angle to the ground. This time when he lands his front right hoof comes down hard between two rocks. At first, I don't realize what's happened. From my point of view all I know is that my horse is shaking his body wildly, unable to move.

"He's stuck," Mateo calls.

I look over Major's shoulder. Mateo is right—his foot is wedged solid!

"Lead him back," Doug says. "Try to get him to work it out."

I do what I'm told, gently pulling back on the reins to guide Major backwards. But he can't pull free.

"Hold on!" Doug calls. "I'll help."

But Major is tired of waiting. In full on panic mode, he tries to rear his way out. And when the rocks still don't give, he loses his balance. Suddenly, I'm falling to my right.

"Watch it!" Oliver cries.

"Jump!" Rusty calls.

Somehow, I get my feet out of the stirrups. I roll free just as Major crashes to the ground. We all hear it: the loud crack. As Major whinnies, everyone is off their horses. When Noah and Mateo manage to wrench Major's leg from the rocks, we see what we had all feared.

It's dangling, broken clean in half.

Chapter 21

"Tie the horses to a tree and stay here," Doug commands, leaping back on Copper.

"Where you going?" I ask.

He's already galloping up the incline to the road.

"To get help! Just keep Major comfortable."

We're shocked, that goes without saying, I guess. Still, we do what we can. First, Garth and I pull off our sweatshirts and make a pillow under Major's head. Then we take turns stroking his mane. We even sing him some camp songs. Then the singing fizzles and we wait, sprawled out on the ground, too upset to say much of anything. It's scary. The most powerful animal most of us has ever seen up close is down and helpless.

"What do you think they're gonna do with him?" Noah asks, eventually.

"Don't know," Rusty says. "Maybe try and set his leg."

"No way," Oliver says. They are the first words he has spoken since the accident. "They'll put him down."

"What?" I say.

Because of Caramel I had known it was a possibility but not one I'm ready to put into words. Even Oliver can tell that he's pushed too hard.

"I don't know," he says with a shrug. "That's what they do to racehorses, right?"

I know it's true. But can't doctors do anything these days? There has to be a way to set the leg of a horse, right? With nothing else to do to make Major comfortable, I finally realize what he'll like the best. Not a sweatshirt-pillow or a round of camp songs, but Merrylegs. I untie her bridle from a nearby tree and let her stand next to him. It's hard to know what she understands but after looking her stricken partner up and down, she nuzzles him once, then stays by his side, watching over him. The rest of us continue to wait, drawing in the dirt with sticks, throwing pebbles, lost in our own thoughts. But soon enough—faster than I had expected, actually—Doug returns, riding Copper wildly down the incline.

"Help is on the way," he says. "I spoke to Harvey. He's calling a vet."

Doug jumps off of Copper, looks more closely at Major's leg and shakes his head, almost like part of him has held onto a hope that it would have healed in his absence.

"I'll stay with Major," he says. "Rusty: you lead the rest of the guys back to camp."

By that point, my cabinmates are all too willing to leave. Being around Major is taking a real toll on the group. Then again, who wouldn't be affected by the sight of a downed horse, hoping for a miracle?

As everyone else gets on their mounts, I look around blankly.

"Who do I ride?" I ask Doug.

"Stay with me, okay? In a few minutes I'll want you to go

up to the Antique Road and guide Harvey and the vet down here when they arrive."

I nod, honored to be singled out with a job to do. As the others mount up they seem to accept that Doug has chosen me because I know more about horses—or maybe they just realize that I'm his favorite—and ride off without complaint. Only Merrylegs lingers for a moment at the top of the hill, looking sadly down at Major, before allowing Garth to lead her after the others. After everyone else has disappeared, Doug and I sit silently for a minute. Major seems comfortable enough, but who knows what he understands. It's strange to think that such a strong horse can be scared.

"Do I really have to go to the road?" I ask, finally.

"Yeah. Jackson. You do." He pauses. "When Harvey and the vet get here, I'm afraid they're going to have to shoot the horse."

Oliver had been right. I swallow hard.

"Yeah," I manage.

"It's tough," Doug says. "As bad as it gets."

I nod, barely managing to fight tears.

More silence.

Finally, Doug forces a smile. "Okay, then. You'd better get going."

I brush Major's cheek with my hand. And then? Well, Major and I were never that close, but I do it anyway: I kiss him on the cheek, then walk back up the hill without looking back. When I reach the top, I sit on a tree stump by the edge of the road. Five minutes later, a camp van pulls up. Harvey gets out with a man in a flannel shirt and a medical kit.

"Hi, Jackson," Harvey says.

"Hey," I say. "They're down there."

Harvey nods. "Good."

He seems almost unconcerned. *Good*? Is that what he said? "Don't you care about your horses?" I feel like shouting. "What's wrong with you?" But then I remember something: Harvey and the vet are older and have seen the cycle of life reenacted again and again. Putting down a horse is sad, but in the realm of the ordinary.

"Okay, Jackson," Harvey says. "You stay here. We'll be right back up."

The vet nods at me then quickly looks away, as if not wanting to acknowledge what's coming or his part in it. They disappear down the path. Again, I sit for a minute. Then, even though I know it's wrong, I turn back down the path, and stoop behind a rock. Down the hill I see Doug and Harvey stand near as the vet, on his knees, looks over Major's leg. He shakes his head then reaches into his bag, I hope to pull out a splint. Instead, it's what I fear most: a pistol. I shudder. Is this really happening? Is he going to shoot the horse right then and there? I know I should look away but I feel strangely compelled to watch. Not just because it's grisly but out of respect. Part of me I wants to run to Major to hold him while he dies, maybe tell him how much Merrylegs had loved him. But I'm frozen. If I show my head, I'll be sent back up the hill. Besides, I can't bear to be closer. In the end, I can't even bear to look. As the vet walks toward Major, I lurch back up the hill, running like mad. At the top, I crash in a small clearing and look up at the sky. I cry a bit. Then I hear it: a lone gunshot that echoes sharply up the hill then fades out into the trees.

Chapter 22

I'm still sniffling when Harvey and the vet come up the hill. Doug is close behind, riding Copper.

"Come on, Jackson," he says.

I vaguely register Harvey and the vet helping me to my feet, then onto Copper's back behind Doug. With my arms around his waist, we ride back to camp, not saying a word. About halfway there, Doug cries softly for a minute. It feels strange to hear an adult express grief. But also freeing. Doug's tears make me feel less embarrassed about my own.

That night at dinner, Harvey breaks the news to the camp and reads a short prayer in Major's honor. Then he does something thoughtful—he excuses Group 3 from that evening's activity and gives Doug and Scott permission to take us into town for pizza. I have to say that it feels good to bond with the older kids again and talk it all out. Even Joey Ambrose wipes away a tear over dinner, calling Major's death 'tyrannical.' After pizza, I think we're going to head back to camp to see the musical, but the rest of the guys want to stay downtown. Doug takes me aside—he can read my mind—and tells me he'll get a message to the girls camp so that Luna will know it wasn't my fault that I don't show. "There won't be much time to hang out anyway," Doug says. "It's a sit and watch thing."

So that's that. I stay with the guys. We ride bumper cars at a mall, get ice cream cones, then roll back into camp just as Rusty is putting the rest of the cabin to bed by the light of another roaring fire in the cabin fireplace.

As I tuck myself in, Doug sits on the edge of my bunk. He has more to say—something he's been waiting to say in private.

"Listen," he whispers. "What happened today? It wasn't your fault, okay? It was mine."

I swallow hard. Like I said, Doug has a way of reading a person's mind.

"Your fault?"

He sighs, clearly as tortured by what happened as I am. "I never should've stopped at the field by the Antique Road. I should've known better."

"You couldn't have known how crazy the horses would get."

"Yes, I could," Doug says. "I've been there too many times to count. They always go crazy. I wasn't thinking."

"Well, I should've controlled Major."

Doug shakes his head. "No one could've controlled Major today, okay?"

"But..."

"No one," he repeats. "I put you in an unwinnable situation. I was the grown up. I screwed up. I take the responsibility."

I don't know if I believe him or if I'll ever believe him, but it's still nice to hear. The least I can do is return the favor.

"Two misplaced rocks. Major's foot. It was all rotten luck."

"Maybe," Doug says.

"No, it was."

Doug lets that sink in for a moment.

"I was wrong the other day in the pasture, you know."

"When?"

"Walking home after the dance. I said Major and Copper just needed to burn off steam. I didn't believe their feelings were so personal."

"Yeah," I say, remembering. "They both love Merrylegs."

Doug nods in the half light from the fire. "They both did anyway." He sighs. "No guilt, okay? For either of us."

I nod. "I'll try."

"Good then," he says. "I will, too. Now get some rest."

I can't. After everyone has fallen asleep, I'm wide awake, reliving the events of the day. It had been great to go out with Doug and Scott and the gang and nice of Doug to speak to me privately. But every time I try to get sleepy, I find my mind turning to the one person—animal—who needs some attention: Merrylegs. As far as I know she's spent every single minute of the summer with Major. How is she feeling now? Does she know what's happened? That she will never see her true love again? Who is comforting her?

I stay awake for a minute, watching the fire burn down. Then I get out of bed, pull on a pair of jeans and tiptoe out of the cabin. Pete is on duty, but reading a book which makes it easy to sneak by. I can hear a few staff joking around in the Main House but the coast is clear. Walking by the light of the moon, I round the tetherball court, woodcraft area, and barn. That's where I freeze. On the side of the post office there's a shadow: not of a tree or a person—but unless I'm seeing things—of a *horse*. For a split second I think it's Major come back from the dead to haunt me. But something almost even more shocking happens: what I think was only a shadow turns into an actual animal, walking into this sudden pool of moonlight.

"Merrylegs?" I whisper.

As she moves my way, I run to her side and throw my arms around her neck. Yes, I knew she was smart. But smart enough to leave the pasture and walk toward the cabins on her own? Smart enough to come find me? Is that what she's doing? It sounds crazy, but what other explanation is there? The way she rubs her head against mine tells me I'm right. I guess she needs a little comfort, a little company, too. Who knows? Maybe she wants me to know she realizes that it was Major's nature that led to the accident, not my lousy riding. Even so, I have to say it.

"I'm sorry."

I press my face into hers and cry for a quick minute. I'm doing a lot of that lately. When I'm finished, she nuzzles my face. Then I pull gently on her mane and get her moving slowly down the dirt road, past the farm, to the pasture. I'll never know how she's gotten out because the gate is firmly tied shut. When I open it, Merrylegs walks back in with no hesitation, as if she has accomplished what she has set out to do. With only a brief look over her shoulder, she moves toward the infield and disappears into the darkness.

I wait another minute, enjoying the stillness, listening to the wind, imagining Merrylegs heading back to her usual spot, where she's spent every night with Major. Then I turn for the cabin. By the time I get back the fire is embers. I throw in another couple of pieces of wood and blow on the ashes to build it back up. Then I take off my jeans, crawl into my sleeping bag, and watch the flames until I fall asleep.

Chapter 23

I'm woken in the middle of the night by the sound of breaking wood. Rusty is standing by the fireplace, building up the fire. As I stir, I see him prop a two-foot-long branch between the floor and the wall then bring his heel down hard on the middle, splitting it in two. Then he picks up both ends and throws them in the fire, gets down on his knees and blows the embers into a flame. Working quickly, he cracks another branch in half. Then two more and throws them all on the blaze. It's really roaring now, the flames so high they're disappearing up the chimney. Finally satisfied, Rusty takes off his shirt and pants and pulls on his red long johns. Then he sits on his bunk and stares at the fire for a minute. When his eyes circle the cabin, I pretend to be asleep.

When I hear Rusty stand again, I open my eyes. He breaks another largish branch with his bare foot with a loud CRACK! and tosses it into the blaze. Then he collapses on his bunk again. That's when I see Mateo look over the side of the bunk.

"Hey, Rusty," he whispers. "You okay?"

Rusty nods. "Sure, fine. Just building up the fire a bit. Go to sleep, all right?"

"All right."

I see Mateo lie back down, then watch Rusty get up a third time to adjust the fire with his foot. Finally satisfied he crawls into his sleeping bag. Within minutes, he's lightly snoring.

I wait a minute or two, then whisper across the room.

"Hey, Mateo."

Then again. "Mateo."

He sits up in his bunk.

"Jackson? You awake?"

"Yeah, Rusty woke me."

"Me, too. I think he's drunk."

"Really?"

"He looked sort of wobbly."

"Maybe he had a few beers in the pasture with Sami," I say.

"Maybe. Anyway, he's asleep now."

We both look to Rusty, listening to another couple of snores to confirm it.

"So," Mateo says. "You awake enough to talk a minute?"

"Sure. What's up?"

"I'm sorry about Major...I just wanted to say that."

"Thanks," I say. "Me, too."

We pause for a moment, maybe out of respect, I don't know.

"It wasn't your fault, by the way," Mateo goes on, finally. "I even heard Lou and Harvey talking about it in the Main House. Everyone knows you did what you could."

"Thanks."

"Sure."

I let that sink in while a piece of wood burns through and

collapses, sending a shiver of sparks up the chimney.

"Anyway, there's something else you should know," Mateo says.

"What?"

"At the show tonight."

"Was it good?"

Mateo shrugs. "It's a musical about Latinos put on by a camp with three Latinos. How good could it be?"

"I hear you," I say.

"I'm talking about *after* the show."

"What happened?"

"Well, it was weird. Emma was hanging out with Phil Finklehopper."

I sit up on an elbow. "What? Oliver's girl? That Emma?"

"That's right."

"And Phil Finklehopper. The pitcher for the team?"

"The same."

"So what happened? Emma dumped Oliver?"

Mateo nods. "Sure seems that way. She wasn't talking to him really. And Oliver seemed pretty pissed—at first, anyway."

"What do you mean *at first*?"

I'm nervous.

"That's what I want to tell you. After Emma walked off with Phil, Oliver started to talk to Luna."

Boy, does that get my attention.

"Oliver and Luna talked? About what?"

"I couldn't hear."

"Did they go off together?"

"No, nothing like that, but Oliver was standing real close to her."

"How close?"

"*Real* close," Mateo says. "Like kissing distance."

Kissing distance?

"But they didn't kiss, right?"

"No, I said nothing happened," Mateo says. "But Oliver likes her again, I can tell. He's probably hoping to make some sort of move at the fair."

"God," I say. "Really?"

"Really. But relax. It's you that she likes."

"You think?"

"I know!" Mateo practically shouts it. Then he lowers his voice back to a whisper. "She took you to the spring and spewed out her whole life story. That's love."

I'm reassured—a little bit anyway. Mostly, I'm pissed at Oliver. After all, he's had his chance with Luna. Sure, she isn't technically my girlfriend, but we have something brewing—something good.

"Oliver is such a jerk."

I guess I feel it needs to be said one last time.

Mateo smiles. "You're just figuring that out now? By the way, he was the one who put Noah's high tops up the flagpole."

"Really? How do you know?"

"Noah found a witness. Some kid from Cabin 6 who got up early to go to the bathroom."

I shake my head. "Noah loves those sneakers. They're like a stuffed animal to him."

"He was so pissed he sat on Oliver for ten minutes," Mateo says.

I laugh. "Really?"

Mateo nods. "And you know that Oliver was the one who put maple syrup in my hair gel."

"Had to be," I say.

"It would be nice get back at him somehow, wouldn't it?" Mateo says. "Just to take him down a notch?"

Bam! Suddenly I have it. Without saying a word, I'm out of bed then climbing the ladder to Mateo's bunk. I know exactly where he keeps his phone, under his pillow.

"What do you want with that?" he asks.

I'm already scrolling through Mateo's photos. When I get to the one I'm looking for Mateo has to cover his mouth to keep from laughing.

One Last Ride

"Oliver?" he says.

"Right," I say. "Play it."

By that time I'm sitting next to Mateo. He presses a button on his phone. It's a three second video tops, but Oliver is dancing and shouts: "Hear this, girls of RBG! Come get me!"

"Funny," Mateo says, "But what can we do with it?"

I smile. "You know everything about this place, Mateo. Is there somewhere to get your phone online? Some rock or tree?"

Mateo is grinning.

"Well...How about right here out my window!"

I blink. That's a shocker.

"What?"

"Why do you think I took this bunk this year? I scoped it out last summer. I stick the phone out the window and I get a signal. It's one of the only places in camp."

"Amazing! What do you do with it?"

Mateo shrugs. "Text now and then with friends, but mostly nothing. It's just nice to know it's there—a connection with civilization, you know. So yeah, I can get you online. What do you want to do?"

I can barely keep my voice steady, I'm so excited.

"Can you download something onto RBG's facebook page?"

I've never seen Mateo grin more broadly.

"What?" I say. "You can?"

"Oh, I can do better than that!" he says.

"What?"

"Forget Ruth Bader Ginsberg's facebook page. How about the home page of their website!"

"You can do that?"

Mateo holds out his hand.

"Gimme the phone!"

Chapter 24

The next morning, neither Mateo or I say a thing about Oliver's video. To be honest, we don't even know if the download has worked and we sure don't want to give away our involvement if it does. So, we keep our mouths shut. I also keep my mouth shut about Luna, which may be gutless, but I decide that the best strategy for dealing with Oliver's renewed interest is to ignore it. After all, Mateo is usually right. And he said that Luna likes me. For one of the first times in my life I make the choice to be confident.

There's a strangeness in the cabin that morning that makes discussions of girls or pranks seem out of place anyway. Everyone wakes still feeling upset about Major. It isn't until a breakfast food fight involving pieces of bacon, Fruit Loops and orange juice that the tension breaks. We aren't being hard-hearted, I don't think. Odds are that no one who was on that trail ride will ever forget it. But there is only so much stress and sadness a kid can take. The food fight becomes a moment of closure, a way of giving ourselves permission to enjoy the last day of camp.

And it isn't long before Mateo and I have something big to enjoy there and then. Sure, Mateo and I thought his download had gone through. But it still seems a little surreal when we see a Cabin 8 kid hustle into the dining hall and whisper something to Lou, who then gets up and whispers something to Harvey, who, to his credit, begins to grin like a madman. Then just like that—things are moving fast now—another Cabin 8 kid is at our table, whispering to Oliver. As he hears the news, his eyes go so wide they practically explode out of his face.

"What?" he says, finally.

The Cabin 8 kid whispers some more, laughing now. Oliver lurches to his feet. Before Doug or Rusty can stop him, he sprints through the dining hall to the office. By that point word has spread—it did that at camp. The few who know what is going on are laughing like they're possessed while everybody else is desperately asking what is up. Then the office door slams and the dining hall goes stone quiet as Oliver scrambles, I assume, to find a computer to see for himself. We don't have to wait long. A moment later, his voice echoes from the office like a harpooned baboon.

"Nooooo!"

And what happens then? It gets even better because the same Cabin 8 kid who has run into the dining room a moment earlier holds up a laptop—don't ask me how he has it, maybe he keeps it under his pillow like Mateo keeps his phone—and displays Ruth Bader Ginsberg's homepage. Sure, the screen is small, but most people get right away what they were looking at.

Oliver dancing! And then his voice echoes out of the laptop, filling the dining hall:

"Hear this, girls of RBG! Come get me!"

One Last Ride

Then—an explosion. Laughter, hoots and cat calls shake the Main House so hard that I think it will either fall over or take off into outer space. After all, what makes a boy happier than to see another of his breed publicly humiliated? Nothing. It didn't even matter that a second later, RBG's website goes dark, shut down by someone who's noticed that it's been hijacked. That the prank has worked for even a second is enough. The laughter keeps building, coming in waves, rocketing off the walls of the Main House. The only question now is what Oliver will do when he comes out of the office—that is, if he *ever* comes out of the office. For all we know he's sitting in the corner sucking his thumb. That's what I would've been doing.

But that's when I learn once again to never underestimate Oliver Kemp. Just when I think he might've climbed out the window and sprinted all the way home, the office door swings open and there he is. Does he look embarrassed? Not for a second. In fact, the guy is clasping his hands over his head like he's just gone ten rounds in the WWF.

"Yo, everyone!" he shouts. "Nice, right?"

Just like that, jeers and shouts turn to cheers. Oliver is the hero once again, not for his fielding and hitting, but for his *attitude*. The kid even takes a bow!

"Ol-i-ver!" the crowd chants. "Ol-i-ver!"

"Don't worry," Mateo whispers to me. "He's dying inside."

Probably. But walking back to the table, Oliver keeps up the façade, slapping five, accepting congratulations like he's just cured mad cow disease or something. Back at the table he keeps up appearances.

"Good one, guys," he says. "I mean, whoever did that, not bad at all."

"So wait a second," Doug asks for all of us, smiling. "You don't care?"

Oliver waves a hand. "That I was speaking the truth to the girls of RBG?" He grins big. "The way I figure it, they're lucky."

The old Kemp confidence. I mean, I would've been shaking

in a corner, ready to deport to a third world country—and here he is, practically celebrating.

"Well, it serves you right in my opinion," Noah says.

"And why's that?" Oliver asks.

Noah blinks, as if he can't believe Oliver could be so dumb. "For how you murdered my high tops!"

"Ah, so you're admitting it then," Oliver says. "You're who downloaded that video?"

Noah stuffs a piece of sausage in his mouth, once-again instituting the no-chew method. "I'm not saying that at all. I had nothing to do with it. I was sleeping like a dead dog."

It has the ring of truth. When Noah crashes there's no waking him.

"So who then?" Oliver asks. He looks around the table. "Come on, it was a good prank, I want to congratulate whoever thought it up."

I don't believe him for a second. Congratulate whoever did it? More like punch whoever thought of it in the face.

"Wasn't me," Rusty says.

That made sense, too. Why would a counselor with three girlfriends care enough to prank a camper? Something like that could get him fired.

"Me either," Garth says, looking up from his book. "Pranks are beneath me."

We buy that, too—Garth is above pretty much anything that doesn't have to do with the life of the mind or elves. That leaves me and Mateo. Oliver is dumb but he isn't anybody's idiot.

"So what of it, Mateo?" he says. "You're the one with the phone, right? I mean, everyone knows it."

Mateo takes it in stride, stuffing a bite of muffin in his mouth.

"So what?" he says. "Sure, I have a phone. But I never took a video of you doing anything. If you don't believe me, check my photos."

"Aw, you've erased it already," Oliver says, correctly.

One Last Ride

"No proof then," Mateo says. He takes a swallow of orange juice. "Just like there's no proof you put maple syrup in my hair gel."

Oliver plays it innocent. "Me? I didn't do that."

Mateo smiles more broadly. "And I had nothing to do with that post."

"Fair enough," Oliver says. "But I am saying this: when I find out who did it, revenge will be secured. Count on it."

That's when I should've kept my big mouth shut.

"Revenge?" I ask. "How?"

Suddenly, all eyes are on me. I guess the question had come out nervous, almost like a confession.

"I'm not saying I did it," I stammer. "I'm just wondering what you would do."

"That's easy," Oliver says, staring me down. "I look for whatever a person cares about most, then attack."

That's it—Oliver Kemp laid bare. So far that summer he had attacked Mateo's hair and Noah's high tops. For all I know he had ripped out pages from some of Garth's books, too. So what did I care about most? Luna, that's who.

"Hey," I say, as forcefully as I can. "Stay away from her."

"Who?" Oliver asks.

The kid is toying with me.

"You know who," I say.

"Luna?" Oliver says. "What of her?"

Out spills the whole thing. "What of her? I heard you were talking to her last night."

The table goes quiet. Obviously, everyone else had known but hadn't known that I had found out. Of course, Oliver doesn't back down. Not that I expect him to.

"Sorry, bud. But I'll talk to whoever I want when I want!"

I guess he says it with enough of an edge that Doug feels he has to put a stop to things.

"Hey, guys. Settle down, all right?"

Doug is gentle but commands respect, even from the Oliver Kemps of the world. So we both mumble all right and the subject is dropped. But when Oliver grins at me from across the table as Rusty is scraping plates, I know: this isn't over.

Chapter 25

Later that morning, Michelle finds me in the main yard. For a split second, I think she's finally going to confront me about what I had seen at her cabin. Was she there to take me outside to be worked over by Jay Kreigel? Maybe knit me into a rug?

"Hey, Jackson," she says. "We heard from your folks."

I'm so preoccupied with everything else I've almost forgotten.

"Oh, really?" I say.

She nods. "Yes, your mom sent an email. She said they'd be here tomorrow at eleven to get you."

I blink. "She said *they'd* be here? Like both of them?"

Michelle smiles. She knows what's at stake. "Honestly, the email didn't go into a lot of detail. Just that they'd be here. I guess that means both of them, right?"

I smile back. Of course, that still doesn't mean that they aren't getting divorced. For all I know they're driving up together to break the news. Who knows? On the other hand, it has to be a good sign, right?

"Yeah," I say. "Thanks."

Michelle touches my hand. "Hey, have a great last day."

So I decide to do just that.

That morning, Group Three rides together for the final time. Given Major's terrible accident, we're more low key than usual, but only for a couple of minutes. We take the horses to the pasture, four boys and Doug and Scott. And for the first time that week, I get to ride Merrylegs and even make the last tag of the day, galloping up from the lower pasture to nab Barry on Gidget by first base. Then all sweaty from riding on a day that has turned sunny, I head to the pond for eleven o' clock swim. After taking turns with some other kids jumping off the diving board into the deep end, the day takes another good turn. In the distance is a dark haired girl on a kayak. As she draws closer I realize who it is: Luna!

"Hey!" she calls. "I'll see you tonight, okay?"

Sometimes life gives you boosts you hadn't realized you needed. Despite Mateo's certainty that Luna still likes me I've remained stressed that my failure to go to the musical and Oliver's renewed interest has destroyed whatever chances I have with her at the fair. But her big-gummed grin is so welcoming that I take a risk and lay all my cards on the table.

"Absolutely," I call back. "Can't wait!"

She smiles even wider and waves. No way that girl likes Oliver. I have nothing to worry about.

Lunch is good that day, too, spaghetti and meatballs, a camp favorite that even our taste-challenged cooks can't screw up. Then it's time to prepare for the fair. How it works is this: Every Flying Eagle and RBG cabin is required to run some sort of booth that campers pay to use with a pocketful of dried white beans that are dispensed beforehand. I find out that some cabins have annual traditions: Cabin 6 always turns the woodshop into a haunted house. Cabin 7 runs Dunk the Counselor. The oldest cabin at RBG, Killington, sets up a jail of chicken wiring by the post-office where campers can lock up friends and enemies (briefly) for a price. And of course, Cabins 8 and 9 convert the nature room into their teenage version of a bachelor pad-love den, complete with psychedelic music, black-light posters, throw pillows, root beer, dancing, and the famous covered table.

Though Harvey has advised counselors and campers alike to start thinking about their booths a good week earlier, Cabin 3 has let it slide until the last minute. During rest hour, after a brief appearance by the four-legged Harvey Jones, we get down to it. All seven of us, campers and counselors, are lying in our bunks.

"Let's do a thing where people throw darts at balloons," Noah suggests.

"And spend all night blowing up balloons?" Oliver calls over. "I'd rather be ripped apart by a skunk."

It's a good point.

"We could have a quiz booth," Garth says, looking up from an ever-present book. "Ask people questions."

"Questions?" Oliver says. "About what? One of your elves? That'd be idiotic."

Another idea dismissed.

"I know!" Noah says, jumping to the floor. "We get Harvey Jones—the chipmunk—to do a performance. He likes my trunk, right? So here's what we do. We capture him then bring the trunk and Rusty's radio to the main yard and get people to pay to see him dance."

For a second we assume that Noah is kidding, until the exact second that we all realize that he isn't.

"That dance was a one shot deal," Rusty says, lying back on a mountain of pillows.

"And Harvey doesn't work outside the cabin," I say. "We all know that."

Actually, I don't know that—I have no idea what Harvey Jones does outside of rest hour—but what are the odds of catching a chipmunk and getting him to dance on command?

"Sorry," Mateo says. "Doesn't work."

"A real dumb idea," Oliver adds.

"Do you have anything better?" Noah asks. "Does anyone?"

Which is when I see it, sitting there smack in the middle of our cabin. Once a week, every cabin dumps their dirty clothes into a white laundry bin that measures about five feet long, three feet across and four feet high. Once filled, the bins are collected by tractor, transferred to a van and driven into town. Magically, the clothes come back late that afternoon, warm, clean, and folded.

"I have something better," I say. "But it might be a little bit crazy."

"Crazier than a disco-dancing rodent?" Oliver asks.

"Maybe."

"What?" Rusty asks.

I sit up in my bunk. "You know what I've always wanted to do? Get into one of those laundry bins with wheels on the bottom then ride down a hill."

"That *is* crazy," Noah says.

"It was just an idea, okay?"

"Maybe not a bad one," Mateo says.

"What?" Noah says. "You're joking."

"I'm not," Mateo says. He turns to me. "How would you get them on?"

"Get what on?" Garth asks.

"The wheels."

I shrug. "I don't know. Screw 'em on, I guess. Get Pete to help us."

Noah sighs. "Okay, but even if that could work, where would we ride them?"

I haven't really thought it through. "Down the hill from the flats to the main yard?"

One Last Ride

"That's insane," Noah says.

"Actually, it sounds like fun."

To my surprise that's Doug, calling over from his bunk. I haven't even known that he's been listening—he usually dozes or gets lost in his guitar during rest hour.

"Really?" I ask.

"Sure. The trouble is that the bins would probably tip over."

Another roadblock. Then more help comes from another unexpected quarter: Oliver.

"Not if we made a track so they stayed straight."

"A track?" I ask.

"We could do that, actually," Garth says.

"How?" Mateo says.

"Use benches," Garth says. "Or logs even."

Suddenly, my crazy idea has possibilities, however remote. I find myself imagining the moment when I take Luna by the hand to give her the honor of the first ride.

"Sounds worth further exploration to me," Doug says.

"Sure would be original," Rusty says.

"Wait!" Noah says. "You guys can't really be considering this!"

Rusty ignores him. "If you can get Pete to put wheels on the bottom of a few of those bins, you might be in business."

"It'd be better than a stupid dart throw," Oliver says grudgingly.

"Forget the darts," Rusty says. He turns to me. "Go find Pete and ask if he thinks it can work."

"Sounds about right," Doug says. "Go ask and report back. We'll wait."

It's hard to believe I had gotten that far, especially when I've been half joking. But I sprint to the main yard where Pete is already hard at work, helping to set up the chicken wiring for the make-shift jail.

"Hey, Jackson boy," he says. "You look to be a kid with something on his mind."

"An idea," I say. "Maybe a crazy one."

"I'm listening," he says.

"Do you think you can screw wheels to the bottom of a couple of laundry bins for a ride for the fair?"

Pete doesn't answer, not right away, that's not his style. Instead, he looks slowly toward the barn.

"You mean to roll down a hill, I'm guessing?"

"Right."

"So they don't fall over and no one gets hurt?"

"Well, yeah."

Pete is silent another moment. And then...a grin.

"What?" I ask. "We can do it?"

Pete turns back to the chicken wire jail.

"Haul a few of 'em up here and we'll see what we can do."

With special permission, the boys of Cabin Three round up four laundry bins and haul them to the main yard. Pete is already ready for us with some small wheels he's found in the toolshed.

"Let's see now," he says. "Flip one of those over."

We do as we are told. Luckily, they're held together on the bottom by wooden strips. For someone as handy as Pete, it's pretty simple to screw a wheel per corner into the wood. Once that's done, we walk up the path I had taken to reach Sunrise a few days earlier and survey for the best route down to the main yard. Ultimately, we decide on a straight shot from the lower tennis court to the bench in front of the main house. By the time rest hour is over word has spread. To my surprise, Greg, Barry, and Joey come over to lend some muscle to the enterprise.

"Cabin Three and Group Three," Greg says. "That has a nice ring to it."

No argument from me. First, we grab shovels and rakes and smooth the path. Then we make a series of make-shift guard rails out of benches, logs, and a wrecked ping-pong table. At the finish line we amass a pile of hay (borrowed from the ranch) and a few pillows from the Lost and Found. By the time we're done, it's four o' clock swim.

"Who's going to take the first ride?" Pete asks.

"Two of us should be able to fit pretty easily," I say. "I'll go."

"Me, too," Mateo says.

That seems about right. Mateo and me, best friends, first to risk our lives on my dream ride.

"All right," Pete says. "In you go."

I climb in first and sit with my legs crossed. Mateo comes in after and wraps his legs around mine, like a bobsledder.

"Lemme know when you're ready?" Pete says. "I'll give you a push."

A pretty big crowd has formed by then, mostly gathered in the main yard by the finish line. Obviously, most kids aren't there to see a raging success but a giant, spectacular failure, perhaps featuring a crash where Mateo and I get medivacked to the nearest hospital. To be honest, that's what I half expect, as well. But Mateo? He's raring to go.

"Let's get this show on the road," he cries. "Someone give this sucker a push!"

Before I know it, the crowd goes quiet. Out of the corner of my eye, I see Pete stretch his leg.

"Ready, boys?"

"Ready!" I say.

I grip the front of the basket. Pete gives us a hard kick...we roll an entire yard then stop with a jolt. Laughter carries so forcefully up the hill I think it might blow me out of the bin.

"Nice one, Jackson!"

"Good ride, Cabin Three!"

"What? You guys are gonna charge people to sit in a laundry basket?"

As the laughter peaks and insults fly, Pete scratches his chin and gets down on his hands and knees.

"See anything?" I ask, nervously.

"Well, I see four wheels."

Not helpful information.

"Any reason they aren't rolling?"

"Well, one of 'em *is* pointing the wrong way."
"One what?" I say. "One wheel?"
"Yep!"
"Can you fix it?"
"Let me see."
Pete takes a wrench and twists the wheel into line.
"That should do it," he says. "Hold tight now."
I barely have time to look back forward before he gives us another kick, a big one. This time it works. Just like that, Mateo and I are rolling fiercely down the hill, bouncing wildly, picking up speed.
"Yes!" I cry.
Close to the flat of the main yard, we knock against one of the guard-rails—the ping-pong table—then straighten out and careen toward the finish, barreling into the main yard until bam!—we hit a rock and flip out of the bin smack into the pile of hay and pillows.
The applause is explosive.
"Whoo hoo!"
"Nice ride!"
"My turn!"
"Me next! Me!"
Suddenly, there's a race up the hill to the starting line—and the fair isn't due to start for three more hours. Leave it to Oliver to keep order.
"Beat it, idiots. Get your rides at the fair—when you pay!"
We exchange a smile. Don't get me wrong, I'm still worried about what Oliver might do to mess up my night with Luna, but at that moment we're on the same team. And there's still work to be done. I mean, it won't do to have the basket catapult its occupants after each ride, right? What if they miss the hay and pillows? It'd be total carnage. So the rest of the afternoon is given over to attaching a brake pad to each cart. We work through dinner, going in and out to grab quick bites. And just as we've put up a final barrier (this one from an old bench from the main house) and make sure the brakes are functional—the

rider in the back can pull a rope and bring the cart to a smooth halt—the bell rings.

I gasp. The fair is beginning. I look to the post-office, hoping to see the girls of RBG coming down the dirt road. Maybe Luna can take the first ride? Instead of a camp of girls, I see something else: a bunch of boys, laughing, gathered around a horse.

Merrylegs!

Then I see the sign someone has hastily erected over her... And these are the words:

JACKSON'S KISSING BOOTH

Chapter 26

Jackson's Kissing Booth?
Oliver!
I look. He's laughing.
"Not cool!" I say, stepping toward him.
"I knew what mattered to you most wasn't a girl," he says. "You've always been in love with that horse! So go ahead. Your lady is waiting."
I'm stunned, embarrassed. The blood is pounding in my ears.
"You took Merrylegs out of the pasture?"
I still can't believe it. Then I realize I haven't seen Oliver in the last half an hour—plenty of time to grab Merrylegs and put up the kissing sign.
"Oh, relax. It's just a stupid horse!"

"A stupid horse?" I say.

Oliver laughs. "Hey, everyone," he shouts, pointing at Merrylegs. "Look at Jackson's bitch! Go ahead," he says, turning to me. "Kiss her, right on the lips."

Do I need to tell you that I don't need to hear anything else? Jackson's *bitch*? I'm on him in a second, fists flying. Oliver is so surprised that I get in a punch or two before he begins to fight back. Then he has me on my back on the ground and then Doug and Rusty are breaking us up. I'm crying by then. Because of what Oliver did, of course. But also because of everything else that has been going on, too. Yes, my parents are coming to get me but that doesn't guarantee a future together, does it? And yes, Luna seems to like me, but that doesn't guarantee that she won't stand me up or go off with Oliver at the last second, does it? And now my favorite horse has been used for a dumb prank by the cabin monster? It's all too much for a guy like me to take. Sure, Merrylegs doesn't seem to mind—she stands there calmly like she always does—but that's not the point. There's a principle at stake.

"He took Merrylegs out of the stable!" I shout to Doug. "Did you see that sign he wrote?"

I lunge back to Oliver but Rusty holds me tight. That's when Doug takes over.

"Horses aren't toys, Oliver," he says, voice cold. "Come on now. Take down the kissing booth sign then lead Merrylegs back to the pasture. Get her a bale of hay, too."

Oliver frowns.

"A bale of hay? It was just a dumb prank. I didn't mean anything by it."

"Looks to me like you meant quite a bit by it," Rusty says.

"Come on!" Oliver goes on. "I'll take down the sign but if I walk back the horse I'll miss the beginning of the fair!"

"Now!" Doug says.

"Damn!" Oliver says.

That's when I realize something. There's no way on this planet that I'm going to let Oliver near Merrylegs—not if I can help it. I don't want his dirty hands touching her. If anyone is going to take care of my horse it's going to be me.

"No," I say. "I've got this."

I shake Rusty loose, but instead of moving toward Oliver I start toward Merrylegs.

"Jackson," Doug says. "You don't have to."

"I know," I say. "I want to."

After all, who knows if Merrylegs will be back next summer? Who knows if *I* will back? I might never see her again. So I walk past a group of smirking boys and stroke her mane.

"It's okay, girl," I say. "I'll lead you back. It'll just take a second."

Then I get a surprise—a big one.

"Okay if I help?"

I look up. There's Luna, leading the pack of RBG campers. I try not to show how happy I am to see her. So I nod and maybe smile a little. Then I grab Merrylegs' halter. The crowd parts and Luna and I walk side by side, past the rest of the RBG girls coming down the hill, back up the dirt road to the ranch.

"Jackson's bitch, huh?" she says.

"Yeah. Real creative, right?"

Luna sighs. "Oliver's a real wit, that's for sure."

I smile. "Yep."

Then I realize something. I can't be sure how long Luna has been watching but most likely she had seen the entire scene. Which meant she had seen Oliver flip me on my back like I was ninety. Not good.

"He sure kicked my butt, though," I say. "Or he would've if Doug and Rusty hadn't stepped in."

Luna laughs. "Fighting over a horse?"

I shrug. "Yeah. Why not?"

"Well, I think it's sweet."

I don't respond, maybe because I'm blushing, but it feels good to hear that. We walk the rest of the way to the pasture in silence. Then I get a bale of hay and we spread it out for all the horses. It actually doesn't take more than a few minutes.

Then I give Merrylegs a quick hug.
 "Sorry, girl," I said.
 "Come on," Luna says. "The fair."
 She's holding out her hand. I take it, of course.

Chapter 27

We run half the way back then walk a bit to catch our breath, then run the rest of the way. I know what I wanted to show her first. When we get back to the Main Yard and up the hill by the tennis courts, Mateo is taking beans for our ride.

"Whoa!" Luna says. "What the heck is this?"

"A laundry bin," I say.

"It was Jackson's idea," Mateo says.

He shoots me a quick wink. Patti is there, too, standing by his side.

"Really?" Luna says.

"It's cool," Patti says. "I've been twice already."

"Great," Luna says. "I'm in."

She reaches into her jean pocket, ready to pay. Time for

the grand gesture.

"No," I say. "For you, free."

And so Mateo helps Luna into the bin. I get in behind and tuck my legs around her.

"I hope this next part is okay," Mateo says with a smirk. "Because Jackson's going to have to put his arms around your waist."

"Luna'll just hate that," Patti says.

"I'll deal with it," she says.

We get in and I wrap my arms around her. To top things off, I hold her close and clasp my fingers. To tell the truth, I could've sat there all night. Maybe even stayed in that laundry bin all year until the next season. As it is, Mateo gives us a sudden push and we're off. There's not much to say about the ride itself except that it's fast and Luna screams—not out of terror, at least I don't think so, but pure joy. As for me, I enjoy the speed, of course, but also how the forward motion pushes Luna and me even closer together. Let's hear it for centrifugal force! The next thing I know we're rocketing onto the main yard and into the hay and pillows.

Stationed down below, Garth helps us out then pulls the cart back up the hill. And you know who's there, helping him? Florence! And boy are they jabbering away.

I look to Luna.

"Garth and Florence?" I ask.

She laughs. "Why not? When you think about it, they're perfect."

I have to admit that I'm slightly relieved that Florence has found someone. Anyway, over the next two hours, Luna and I spend nearly every minute together. We visit the haunted house (best effect: a chain saw attached to a fake neck with ketchup for blood), Dunk the Counselor (I get to put down Jay Kriegel twice), the Hay Ride (a trailer of hay pulled by the four speed tractor up to the pasture and back), the Balloon Toss (Cabin One takes that one), and every other booth or ride at the fair. In between, we take breaks to help with our own cabins. While Luna trots off to help with Shrewsberry's cardboard box maze, I man the top of the laundry bin starting line, helping kids on and off, while modestly accepting compliments along with handfuls of beans—until one of the wheels finally flies off one of the bins, flipping two older campers hard onto the grass. They're okay but Harvey Jones shuts us down anyway. "Too dangerous," he says. "Rolling laundry carts? I should never have allowed it." But it's okay. By that time, most of the kids in camp have given it a ride—and Luna and I have gone twice.

All in all, a great night.

But as the fair draws near its witching hour, there's a certain place Luna and I have not visited—the attraction where dreams are granted, where an already perfect day can be taken to an even higher level. From the very start I've wanted to get her into what Cabin 8 and 9 have decided to call "DRINK, DANCE, and DANGER" in the worst way but the prospect of facing the now-mythic make-out table stops me every time. Luckily, we have good friends. Mateo being Mateo isn't about to stand around and allow me to miss out on a chance of a lifetime. With a little more than ten minutes left in the fair, he grabs me by the sleeve. Patti does the same to Luna.

"Come on," he says.

"Where we going?" I ask, though of course I know.

"Just follow us," Patti says.

I suspect that they've already made at least one trip there that night—maybe even two or three. For all I know, Mateo has felt Patti up and the famed table is now a shrine in their honor. That's how confidently they march us through a whirlwind of campers and counselors, past Dunk the Counselor, the barn, to the post office, then up the narrow stairway to the Nature Room. Though my heart is thumping with excitement and dread by the time we reach the top of the stairs, one step into that magical room and I wish I hadn't waited so long. To the eyes of this twelve-year-old, the work Cabins 8 and 9 have done is incredible. All signs of plant and animal life, all terrariums and cages, have been tucked who knows where. The lone light bulb that usually shines overhead has been replaced by this wild strobe light. Black light posters of Jimmi Hendrix, Jerry Garcia, and other retro rock stars line the walls. Bean bag chairs are strewn on the floor. There are throw rugs and incense and in the corner older kids are dancing. Then there is the food: a spread of cookies, brownies, popcorn, and root beer, all for the price of a few beans. As for the legendary make-out table, at first I don't even see it! But when I finally spot it in the far corner, it looks so harmless, I almost laugh. It's taken such an important position in my imagination, I half expect it to be lit in neon. Instead it's what Mateo has said: a simple table with a blue blanket draped over its sides. What the heck is so scary about that? Who says I even have to go under it? No one.

"This is so nice," Luna says.

"I know!"

"There he is! Jackson Segal!"

I look up. One of my Group Three friends, Barry Pepper, is working his shift at the food table.

"Barry!" I say.

"Come here. You and your lady need some root beer."

I try to pay. He refuses.

"Group Three beans are no good at Drink, Dance, and Danger," he says with a quick look to Luna.

"Thanks," she says.

And so we drink root beer. No sooner have we finished our cups than Mateo and Patti drag us to the dance floor where someone has cranked some Beatles—like I say, there's a whole retro vibe about the joint. As the opening chords of "I Want to Hold Your Hand" shake the room, Luna throws herself into it with her usual insane energy, moving and shaking with no inhibitions. So I dive in, too—straight into a pit of kids dancing like their lives depend on it, trying to eke every last bit of fun out of the night before the final bell. With a quick glance I see that Mateo, Patti, Luna, and I are the youngest on that dance floor by at least a year, another thrill.

"Yo, Segal!"

Joey Ambrose, dressed in yellow bell-bottoms and a pink dress shirt, appears out of the mix, holding hands with a girl at least a year his elder.

"Yo, Ambrose!" I call back. "How you doing?"

"Getting down and tyrannical!" he calls.

Then he smiles and gives me a light punch on the shoulder before shimmying back into the crowd.

"Who's that?" Luna shouts.

"Just a guy in Group Three," I say.

As the words come out of my mouth, Greg is suddenly on our other side, dancing with not one, but two girls.

"Jackson!"

"Greg!"

We slap five and he dances off.

"Another friend?" Luna asks.

I nod. "Yeah."

"You know everyone."

Not true but I sure don't refute it.

As the song crescendos to its grand finale, I WANT TO HOLD YOUR HAAAAAAAAND!, everyone cheers and stamps the floor.

"One more?" Luna yells.

"Absolutely!"

But no sooner are the words out of my mouth than I catch a sideways glance of the table. Is there still time to get a turn underneath? If so, now is the moment, right? With another dance, it might be too late! And then to my horror, I hear something that strikes fear into my heart: the camp bell.

"Oh, darnit!" Luna says.

I sigh, furious, a golden opportunity wasted. The table is so close I can practically touch it!

"I know," I say. "It stinks."

But then...

"Keep dancing!" Joey calls out. "That was just the first bell."

"What?" I say. "Really?"

Joey smiles. "Relax, Segal. We've got at least five more minutes. Make 'em count!"

With that, the opening riff of "Ticket to Ride" blasts through the speakers—more Beatles. I'm ecstatic. Thrilled! More precious time! But how to maneuver Luna to the table? Do I dance her closer then pretend to fall down and push her under or do I just suck it up and ask her straight out? I needn't have worried. As John Lennon sings the opening words, "*I think I'm gonna be sad*," Patti and Joey's girl grabs Luna by the arms. Then suddenly I feel myself being physically lifted off the floor by Greg, Barry, Joey and Mateo.

"What the heck?" I shout.

"Onward!" Joey cries.

The next thing I know I'm being half carried, half dragged to the corner of the room, then roughly deposited back on the floor by the famed piece of furniture.

"Follow us," Mateo says.

He and Patti fall to their knees and scoot under the table.

"You guys next," Greg says.

Luna and I exchange a glance. Out of the corner of my eye, I see another couple—a kid in Cabin 4 and a girl from RBG—move away to the dance floor. It's hard to tell, but it seems like they've decided they aren't quite old enough, brave enough, or whatever enough to go under the table. I'm not sure I am either.

"So?" I say to Luna. "What do you think?"

She seems as nervous as I am but manages a sort of smile.

"It might be fun, right?" she says.

"Yeah," I sputter back. "I mean, it's only a stupid table."

With that, she smiles wider then slides under. Is my heart bunny-hopping in my chest? Yep, but there's no backing out now. With a deep breath, I hit the floor and slide through the blanket myself. To my surprise, two people are there I don't expect: Oliver and Emma! And old Oliver? He acts like nothing is wrong. And maybe it isn't. Because as I slide in, he leans into me.

"Sorry about your horse," he says. "Lou just gave me a major tongue whipping. I went too far."

I blink. Can it be? An Oliver Kemp apology? I guess there's a first for everything.

"You're in a good mood for some reason," I whisper back.

Oliver nods. "Because of your prank."

"My prank?"

Oliver smiles. "Yeah, putting up that video. Don't deny it, I know it was your idea."

"Yeah, well," I admit. "What of it?"

"Emma saw it, that's what!"

I choke back a laugh.

"That's why she wanted you back?"

Oliver shrugs. "She said she saw me on the website. Must've liked my confidence." Then he nods at Luna. "Fun fair, right?"

By that point, Mateo and Patti have staked out ground on their own blanket across Oliver and Emma, also side by side. With limited space left, Luna and I are lying across from each other.

"Yeah," I say. "Fun."

Oliver grins big.

"And it's about to get better."

With no further sweet talk, he leans toward Emma and plants one on her lips. Despite the fact that kissing is the table's prime purpose, Oliver's speed stuns me. Even more, the guy doesn't stop at a single peck. No, he and Emma begin to kiss like they know what they're doing, like they've done it before. That's sort of okay, because Emma is fourteen. But then, to my alarm, Mateo and Patti follow suit. For a second, Luna and I watch, dumbstruck. I swallow hard, trying to fight back my dry mouth. I look to Luna. Time to make my move, right? But then...another bell!

"Okay, that one matters," someone cries, a counselor whose voice I don't recognize. "Time to wind things down."

Luna looks over her shoulder then back at me. A second passes that feels like a minute. To come this far and not make an attempt? That would be terrible. So I take a deep breath.

"Can I...?" I ask.

Luna blushes—at least that's how it seems, it's hard to tell in the half light. Then she looks to Oliver and Emma and Mateo and Patti.

"Sure," she says. "But maybe we could start a little more G rated?"

Works for me.

"A single kiss?" I say.

She nods. But then...disaster! As Luna sits up on her knees, I go in too quickly, not to mention with my mouth too far open. Instead of connecting with Luna's lips, I catch a giant mouthful of hair! Worse, a strand gets stuck in my teeth.

"Oh, man," I say.

"Ouch!" Luna calls. "Hey!"

"Sorry."

To her credit, Luna forces a smile. Totally mortifying, but it turns out catching her hair in my teeth has its advantages. It forces her head close to mine.

"Open wide," she says.

I do as I was told. Working carefully, but quickly, Luna extracts her hair.

"Now," she says. "Hold on a minute."

I watch as she pulls her hair behind her ears. When she's done, she slides an inch closer and looks me square in the eye.

"Try again?" she asks.

I go more slowly this time and she's ready. When our lips touch they make a perfect, almost textbook, smack. Then we pull apart, a bit dumbfounded, as if we can't conceive how something so simple can feel so good.

"Wow," Luna says.

"Yeah," I repeat.

I lean in to kiss her again when someone pounds the table top.

"Whoever is in there, time to get out!"

Luna and I gasp.

"All right, everyone! Time for RBG to get back home. Fair's over!"

"It's your dad!" I whisper.

"I know," she mouths back.

We break up laughing, so loudly I'm sure he hears. But as he had at the costume cabin and the sleep out Lou gives us our space. Without another word, he walks out of the room and down the steps.

"We should get going."

To my surprise, that's Oliver.

"Yeah," Mateo says. "I guess we should."

Had he felt Patti up? I have no idea. At that point, I don't care. He kisses Patti a final time then crawls out. We follow one by one.

Back in the main yard, Luna and I hold hands, smiling exactly like twelve-year-olds who have just kissed for the first time are supposed to smile—really really big. It had only been a single kiss. Mateo and Patti's record is safe. But it's enough for us.

"Okay! Ruth Bader Ginsberg! Time to head back."

That's Mrs. Davenport calling from up the dirt road to the farm.

"Text me?" Luna asks. "Email maybe?"

"Sure. Will you?"

She nods. "Absolutely."

I don't care who's around. I kiss her again.

"All right, lovebirds," a voice says. "Break it up."

It's Rusty, smiling. Patti grabs Luna's hand and drags her up the path.

"Bye!" Luna calls. "Text me! Don't forget!"

"I will!"

"Promise!"

"Yes!"

As she disappears up the road, a bunch of Cabin Nine kids

pick up Harvey Jones and drop him in dunk-the-counselor with a loud splash. As the camp breaks into applause, Mateo tackles me. We roll in the dirt, wrestling and laughing, and then I see something else—something pretty significant. Noah, walking hand and hand with a kid from Cabin Seven! Just to be clear: a boy!

I look to Mateo.

"Gay but currently inactive?"

"Not anymore, I guess," Mateo says.

We smile, happy for Noah, but mostly still happy for ourselves.

"Come on," Mateo says.

We sprint, shouting, all the way back to the cabin.

Chapter 28

No boy likes to pack. But the good news is this: since boys are so sloppy, the job doesn't take long. Just shove the clothes and other junk in the trunk and be done with it. Luckily for me and the rest of my bunkmates, Cabin Three's laundry had been returned two days earlier, meaning most of our clothes are clean and folded, making things even easier. The rest of my job entails stuffing in a couple of pairs of shoes, my riding boots, a flashlight, assorted unused batteries, a canteen, and some books. My sleeping bag, blanket, pillow, and dirty laundry go into a duffel bag.

Noah had woken at the crack of dawn to catch a bus back to Boston, saying a quick goodbye, taking along his row of high tops. Though Mateo tells him how we saw him holding hands, Noah just smiles. For once all summer he's strangely quiet. I guess some things are too special to blab about.

Anyway, with my packing done, I have a good two hours left to hang after breakfast with the rest of the guys before parents begin to arrive at eleven. Boys aren't generally big on goodbyes, but as we give the cabin a final sweep and straighten up, we do take some time to chat. I'm all too happy, of course, to rehash the events of the day before. Even though my ride had been shut down as a menace to the public welfare, it was still the talk of the fair. More important was the time under the table. Though Oliver and Mateo are quick to point out that Luna and I have barely begun to explore the world of kissing, I'm happy enough to just have a toehold in the territory. As it turns out, Mateo hadn't had the guts to give Patti a feel and had to settle for breaking his make-out record. But for me? Two quick smacks on the lips? The boy who had arrived at camp earlier that summer could not have imagined such success.

"Not a bad summer all in all," Mateo says.

"Got some good reading done anyway," Garth says.

"Wait," I say. "What about Florence?"

Garth shrugs. "We exchanged email addresses. She has some interesting articles on photosynthesis she wants to share."

With that, he buries his head back in his book. Conversation over.

"You were a good group, guys," Rusty said. "I'll tell you, I've had some bad ones."

"I loved it here," I say, simply.

Again, the pre-summer me could never have anticipated something so sickening coming from my mouth. I'm not the only one. I doubt the pre-camp Oliver would have anticipated what he said next.

"You know what?" he says, gruffly. "I'm going to miss you stupid guys."

We all let that sit for a moment. After everything I've been through with Oliver, it's surprising that in a strange way I'll miss him, too.

"We can always email each other," I say.

"Email?" Oliver says. He laughs. "Are you out of your mind?"

No, Oliver Kemp isn't going to email or text or post on Instagram. Deep down, I know that none of us will. We'll miss camp for a few days, maybe even a few weeks, but soon enough we'll get caught up in school and our friends from back home.

Thankfully, there's another hour or two with this particular set of friends, and I still look forward to reliving some of the fair's glory. But just as I'm about to angle the conversation in that direction, Harvey Jones, the director, enters in the cabin. Strangely, he doesn't seem to have interest in any of us. Instead, he quickly nods our way then signals for Doug to join him outside.

"What's up?" Mateo asks.

"Nothing important," Harvey says. "I just need a word with Doug."

Out they go. Seeing the real Harvey Jones brings his namesake to mind.

"Hey," Mateo asks. "If we tape our names and addresses to our bunks, do you think he'll write us?"

"Who?" Oliver asks.

"Our mascot."

"I hope so," Rusty says. "I'd love some updates on the state of the cabin during the winter."

"Hate to tell you but chipmunks don't know how to write," Garth says, looking up from his book.

"Harvey Jones?" Mateo says. "I wouldn't put anything by that little sucker."

"He sure can dance," Rusty says. "We know that."

"He could find a computer then jump on the keys," I say.

Oliver laughs. "No way, Segal. A typing chipmunk? Not a chance."

It's hard to argue. I have to admit that computer-use does

seem out of reach even for a rodent with Harvey's skills. All other comments on the subject are cut short, however, when Doug reappears.

"Hey, guys," he says.

I notice it right away. He has the same smile and gentle manner. But there's a tightness to him; two lines I have never noticed before are etched on his forehead.

"Everything okay?" Mateo asks.

Doug smiles. "Sure, fine."

Then he calls my name. To my surprise, Doug is at his bunk pulling on his riding boots, suddenly looking like his old self, too, lines of worry gone.

"Yeah?" I say.

"What do you say we go on a final ride?"

"What?" In truth, I've already tucked the horses away in a corner of my mind. My riding days are over—at least until the next summer. "Aren't the horses getting picked up today?"

"Not until tomorrow, actually," Doug says.

"Just you and me?"

Doug smiles. "Unless you object. I thought it would be nice to take a final run." He pauses. "Maybe on the Antique Road? Sound good?"

I swallow hard. Of course it sounds good! It's the one ride I had always wanted to take—a ride that I'd thought would have to wait a long winter.

"Parents don't arrive until eleven," Doug goes on. "That gives us plenty of time."

"Don't be an idiot, Segal," Oliver says. "Go!"

Doug stands. "We'll be back to say goodbye before everyone's folks arrive, okay?"

"Okay," I say. "Let's do it."

Chapter 29

I follow Doug through the main yard, down the dirt road. Along the way I can't shake what happened back at the cabin.

"What did Harvey want before?" I ask as we walk past the farm. "He looked sort of weird."

"He is sort of weird," Doug says. "But he just wanted to remind me to have the stables cleaned out by late afternoon."

That also sounds out of character. Flying Eagle always looks messy, that's part of its charm. And Harvey isn't the type to get after an experienced staff like Doug.

"He didn't chew you out, did he?"

"Oh, no," Doug says. "Scott and I will do a big clean-up later today." We're approaching the pasture by then. "So I assume you'll want Merrylegs, right?"

I nod. "Right. How about you?"

Doug laughs. "Sack of crap."

I laugh, too: Strawberry. Doug always had a soft spot for that red horse.

After retrieving a set of halters from the stable, we head to the pasture. Major's absence feels strange on Cowpatty Field. Not that Merrylegs is alone. In fact, Copper has already taken the big horse's usual spot by her side, finally having what he's wanted all summer. As for Merrylegs, maybe she's happy enough to have a new companion? It's hard to tell. In any case, she lets me lead her away from him to the hitching post. Soon both she and Strawberry are saddled up.

"Ready?" Doug says, as we swing on.

I'm more than ready.

"Yep," I say.

"Let's hit it," Doug says.

We edge our way back around the riding ring into the woods, back down the path the cabin had taken two days earlier. It's a beautiful morning, with a touch of fall in the air, the perfect day for a final ride on my favorite horse with my favorite counselor. But after a few minutes on the trail, I ruin it for myself. You see, that's when I realize why Doug has invited me along. At least, I think I do. I can't shake Harvey Jones—why had he come to our cabin? It doesn't make sense for him to make a special trip to tell Doug to clean up—something Doug surely knew to do anyway. And why had Harvey looked so severe when he arrived and Doug so upset when he had returned? There's only one explanation: Harvey had told him something he had found out about my parents. And that something is obvious—my worst nightmare was coming true. At eleven o' clock they would break the news that they were splitting. And now? Doug is giving me a final gift before my life will be changed forever.

Turning though a small field with a stone fence, scenarios begin to spin through my head. I see my dad picking me up with a new girlfriend, a lawyer he's met while working on a

One Last Ride

deal. Or maybe my mom is coming with her boyfriend, a twenty-something personal trainer and life coach. Or maybe all four of them are coming together, my parents and my new step mom and dad? The thoughts come fast and furious as we ride down the same paths and across the same fields as two days earlier, finally coming up on the small field by the Antique Road where Major had fallen, a piece of landscape that temporarily shocks me out of thoughts of my parents. I've been so caught up in the last days of camp that I haven't thought about what has happened to Major's body. Now I see: he's been buried, the grave marked by a large patch of loose dirt.

"Wait," I say.

Doug stops.

"Who buried him?" I ask.

"Harvey hired a few guys from town," Doug says. "Scott and I came out to help."

I'm tearing up by then. I don't know if it's because of Major or because of the news I'm certain to get from one of my parents.

"He was a good horse, Jackson," Doug says. "A passionate horse, that's for sure."

"He sure was."

Then I think of something.

"Hold on," I say and jump off.

Doug doesn't say a word as I pick up a stick then go to the edge of the grave. Then I scratch out the word as best I can: MAJOR. I pause, and then add two more: AND MERRYLEGS. It's hokey, I know that. But with thoughts of my parents parting, it feels good to keep at least one couple together.

"Nice," Doug says.

I shrug. "It won't last more than a day or two."

"But it's there now," Doug says. "Major would like it."

I pause, taking in my handiwork, once again thinking about what's waiting for me back at camp. Then Doug breaks the stillness.

"Whatever happens, promise me that you'll remember something."

"Yeah?"

To my surprise, his eyes are glistening—clearly being back at Major's grave is affecting him.

"You're a good kid. Remember that. Don't let life get you down."

It's obvious now what he's trying to prepare me for—he's that kind of guy, the kind I want to grow up to be. Doug wipes his eyes with his shirt. Then he laughs.

"Should we gallop this road or what?" he asks.

I wipe my own eyes, all too glad to step away from the grave and the emotions swirling through the air.

"Yeah, sure. Let's do it."

I jump back on Merrylegs and follow Doug up the hill. Once we hit the Antique Road, the horses know what to do. With barely a kick we are off. Merrylegs opens up for me and we gallop like I have always imagined. The faster we go, the more I lose myself to the joy of pure motion and raw speed. For those few minutes I'm happier than I have ever been and probably happier than I will be for a while after. Because when I get back to camp a short while later I know that I'll find out that I had been right. My mother will get out of our old Ford—my dad, as it turns out, won't have come—then she'll take me in the lodge where we can be alone.

"Jackson, I have some news," she'll begin. Her voice might crack a bit before she finally gathers herself to get out the words I know are coming. "Your father and I…we've tried so hard…but we just can't. Not anymore."

Knowing that my life is about to be changed forever, Doug has given me a final gift, a once-in-a-lifetime ride.

"Fun, huh?" he asks when we pull up the horses at the end of the road.

There are tears in my eyes, but not because of what I sense is coming with my parents or because of Major's death, but from the exhilarating joy of the ride, how the wind has slapped my face as I ride through the bumps and turns, occasionally shaky in the saddle, but nonetheless flat-out loving this last gasp of boyhood.

"Oh, yeah," I say. "The best."

I take a deep breath of clean Vermont air. Then Doug breaks the silence with the dumbest question I've ever heard.

"Do you want to gallop some more?"

We exchange a smile that soon becomes a laugh.

"Works for me," I say.

After a quick rest, we're off. Yes, I know by then the news waiting for me. But after a summer of intense drama, both traumatic and thrilling, I also know something else: I'm a different kid now with a little something extra in the tank.

"Yee haw," Doug cries.

I whoop and holler all the way back to camp.

Happy, sad, or whatever…I'm going to be all right.

Afterword

While much of ONE LAST RIDE is made up, some of it is based on real events that happened to me around and about the summer of 1972: my first kiss, my parent's divorce, and a tragedy on a trail ride where a horse named simply "He" broke his leg and had to be put down.

In reality, I wasn't on He's back that day, but I was there on another horse, along with around six other campers and my favorite counselor, twenty-year-old Doug Johnson. It was traumatic to witness and obviously the memory of that day contributed heavily to this story. I remember waiting with Doug (just the two of us) for the vet to arrive. I remember Doug kindly telling me to go up the hill so I wouldn't have to see the horse be killed. For years, I remembered that day and my relationship with Doug, a young counselor I admired who I never saw again—and never thought I would see.

Years passed. Thinking back on that day on the trail and my years at camp, I wrote ONE LAST RIDE. Then one day over the summer of 2023, I noticed a group called "Camp Sangamon Alumni" on Facebook with a picture of a rider on a horse from the 1960s. Under the posts was a comment by "Douglas Johnson." I figured it had to be the same person. I wrote him a note. Doug remembered me and I sent him a draft of this book. We soon reconnected over the phone, followed by a long lunch in New Hampshire where we discussed that fateful day on the trail (and much else) for several hours.

Two weeks later I got a package in the mail. To my astonishment, inside were He's bridle and reins! Doug had saved them for fifty years. After meeting with me, he came upon them, mostly forgotten, in his garage—then polished them up and sent them to me as a gift.

Now He's reins (Major in the story) remain with me, hanging in my closet, the memory of a great horse and a memorable and moving summer.

Acknowledgments

There are many people to thank: friends and family who read drafts and supported me along the long road to bringing ONE LAST RIDE to life.

First and foremost, I would like to thank the counselors and kids of Camp Sangamon and Camp Betsey Cox who were this book's true inspiration.

I'm lucky to have many trusty readers, all of whom provided encouragement and support along the way. Big thanks to Chuck Lane, Billy Aronson, Christine Hemp, John Zimmerman, Kevin Brown, Charlie Gordon, Dave Hill, Nora Elish, Herb Elish, Martha Witt, Skeeter Lee, David Hyman, Alley Foster, Matthew Gartner, Mariah Fredericks, Natalie Standiford, Eric Weiner, Doug Johnson, Gabriella Barschdorff, Alex Foster and Peter Nelson.

Thanks to Leslie Pietrzyk for her always insightful, honest comments…and for the surprising gift of the present tense.

Thanks to John Canaday (as ever) for his enthusiasm, guidance, and general brilliance.

Thanks to my brother, Harry, for his very kind words and belief in this book.

Thanks to Emily Rosenblum for the insightful suggestions that helped push the book over the finish line.

Enormous thanks to my exceedingly fine agent Matt Bialer and his assistant Bailey Tamayo. I so appreciate your unending support and loyalty.

Thanks enormously to talented editors Sean Bloomfield and Colton Witte, founders of 10,000 Lakes, for taking a chance on this book and publishing it with such care.

Huge enormous thanks to the brilliant Wendie Moore Wilhide, who did the lovely line drawings at the head of each chapter. I can't thank her enough for her hard work, kindness, and beautiful talent. It was a joy to work with such a good friend—from camp no less!

Extra special thanks to my family: my loving wife and son, Andrea and John, who have listened to me talk about camp for literally years without complaint - and maybe most of all my daughter, Cassie, whose belief in this story made me see its value with new eyes.

And finally special thanks to the fine horses of the 1970s Camp Sangamon stable: Gidget, Banat, Morocco, Echo, Strawberry, Lisa, He, She and the original Merrylegs.

www.ingramcontent.com/pod-product-compliance
Lightning Source LLC
Chambersburg PA
CBHW020541030426
42337CB00013B/938